CHURCHES WITHOUT WALLS

The Mandate of Isaiah 58

"Is this not the fast that I have chosen...
to let the oppressed go free,
and that you break every yoke?"
Isaiah 58:6

John L. Dammarell
Foreword by Tommy Barnett

I dedicate this book to my dear wife. Karilyn, there are not enough words to thank you for all the many hours that you spent reading and rereading this book and for all your words of encouragement during the times when I thought it would never get finished. This book would never have made it to print without your expertise in editing and the many hours of watching me write and then listening to me read portions of the book to you. I am most blessed because of the treasure that you are in my life. You truly are the BEST — my best friend, my lover, my prayer partner, and my cheerleader. I love your faith and I love you with all my heart.

To my children — Howard, Christie,
David, and Charlie.
You were always there for me and we made it
through the storms together! I'm so very proud of
all of you and who you have become. Thank you for
the times you patiently listened to me when I called
you, asking, "Can you listen to what I just wrote?"

To my stepchildren — Jennifer and Theo.
Thank you for your love and acceptance and your
willingness to listen to me and encourage me.

TABLE OF CONTENTS

FOREWORD

"In *Churches Without Walls*, John Dammarell rightly identifies a living, moving church as the agent of hope to those who have no hope, and the key to community transformation. He knows and lives what he writes about; you will be stirred to see your church remove the walls, both inside and outside, to change your community for the better."

Tommy Barnett
Phoenix First Assembly & Los Angeles Dream Center

PRAISE FOR
CHURCHES WITHOUT WALLS

*J*ohn Dammarell not only opens up the world of Isaiah 58 to the church but is also the living example of it. *Churches Without Walls* is a must read for every pastor in America who wants to be a man of the living word.

Pastor Ed Decker
> Author, *The God Makers, Fast Facts On False Teachings, Understanding Islam, My Kingdom Come* and many other books

John Dammarell articulates a theology of a church without walls that makes the concept of spirituality meaningful and understandable for leaders in today's marketplace.

Pastor Gregg Alex
Executive Director, Matt Talbot Center
Seattle, WA.

In the kingdom, there is only one church. We are all one in the body of Christ. Our hurting world is crying for help, crying for His Church to become real, relational and relevant. Crying for our light to "break forth like the dawn" and for healing to appear. Dr. Dammarell inspires us to transform the walls we have constructed around our faith into bridges. Then go out "to loose the chains of injustice and untie the chords of the yoke, to set the oppressed free..." It's time.

R. Brent Christie

Executive Director, Jubilee REACH Center
Bellevue, WA.

As a Christian CEO, I see business as a tool for the Father to use in completing His Great Commission! John Dammarell's **Churches Without Walls** *speaks directly to Christian business leaders everywhere about the responsibility to do God's work on Earth as it is in Heaven. Answering prayers for the Father through our businesses is what the King asks from us everyday!*

Our blessing is the opportunity to participate in THE MOST EXCITING PROJECT OF THE AGES! Father has a specific plan for His children, influencing businesses and cash flows to direct the first fruits or a portion thereof to the harvest of the Kingdom! Father will in turn bless the first fruits with growth, profits, protection, and sustainability.

Having your company investing in the Kingdom with revenue and employees' time is the most exciting Business Development you can participate in!!

Everyday becomes exciting to see what the FATHER will do!! Hear His call, step up in obedience, and watch the fruit of the Spirit begin taking on a life of its own in the community and with your employees!!

This book is inspiring, right on the mark, and well timed for today's Christian Business Leaders!!!

Roger Blier
CEO, Passport Unlimited
Kirkland, WA

There are certain truths that seem to be hidden, yet to be fully uncovered. Josiah discovered this in 2Kings 22:8, " I have found the book of the law in the house of the Lord." Where was it? Was it lost? Perhaps it took such a servant as young King Josiah for God to trust with His precious truth. Through Josiah, beginning in the church, cultural reform took place.

John Dammarell has written a book that opens up for us the heart of God. Like Josiah, John has made a great "discovery." It is Isaiah 58. Thru the obedience of fulfilling this mandate to the church, provision that is sourced in the Divine, the realization of prophetic destiny will be accomplished.

Has God placed a mandate, a must-do on your heart? Something for your church, business, family, or personal calling? If so, I highly recommend you not only read, but also study this book. Let the words become a revelation for you. Discover Father's heart for His children and you will discover a passion whose wells never run dry!

Frank Marinkovich, M.D.
Kirkland, WA

Churches Without Walls is a powerful book for churches, individuals and businesses. It cuts through religious posturing and points the reader to the heart of God. If you want to chase significance, read this book. If you want your business to be significant and not just successful, read this book. John Dammarell points the reader clearly, through Isaiah 58, to a passionate life, church and business.

Steve Esau
VP Sales, Passport Unlimited
Kirkland, WA

ACKNOWLEDGMENTS

What went on to make this book become a reality is a story in itself. There have been many individuals who have been an influence to me, and many who were exceedingly instrumental in getting this book to the publisher.

I'm very grateful for my brother, Clair, and his wife, Marilyn, who planted seven churches and have pastored for over 60 years. Clair has always been there to pray with me, advise me, and inspire me to become all that God has purposed in my life.

I am indebted to Geoff Pope who put the final edit on the book and made some great suggestions. A big thanks to Ed Decker, celebrated author *(The Godmakers, My Kingdom Come, Fast Facts On False Teachings, Understanding Islam)* and friend, who was the first to read the draft of my book and gave me countless suggestions on improving it. My eternal gratitude to Pastor Tommy Barnett of First Assembly of Phoenix who read the book and wrote the foreword. Mega thanks to Dr. Frank Marinkovich who read the book, encouraged me to publish it, and endorsed it. I am forever indebted and thankful to Roger Blier, Steven Esau and Richard Mueller, owners of Passport Unlimited, who paid for the publishing of this book and for their many gracious words of encouragement.

A huge thanks to my pastors, Dr. Wendell and Gini Smith of The City Church in Kirkland, Washington, whose vision for the poor inspired and challenged me and whose preaching mentored me to greater levels of faith. A great thank you to Pastor Aaron Haskins, City Networking Pastor at The City Church, Kirkland, Washington, who has been a mentor to me personally in inner city ministries. A most hearty thank you to my many pastor friends whom I have partnered with in serving the less fortunate: Pastors Gregg Alex, John Sauls, Ken Ransfer, Charles Alfred, Bill Demps, Joe Carter, Alfred Roberson, Alvaro Cordova, Jimmie Lee, Washington Talaga, Earnest Williams, and Mark Yeadon. A special thanks to Pastor Sharon Blackburn and Bethel Ministries for believing in the Mandate of Isaiah 58 and opening up their home for the many workshops I conducted. You have all been such a wonderful encouragement to me and truly live the message of this book.

Thanks also to my wonderful friends, too numerous to mention. You have all kept me going with your words, "You can do it."

Last but not least, I thank you for reading this book. I pray that it will inspire you to adhere to the Mandate of Isaiah 58, believing for yourself, and the churches and businesses of your communities, to be those rebuilders and restorers of the streets of your neighborhoods, bringing hope to the hopeless and restoration to the less fortunate.

INTRODUCTION

Our communities are really a reflection of how healthy and vibrant the local church is. In order for transformation to take place in our communities, transformation first needs to take place in the churches of our communities, breaking through racial, denominational and socio-economic boundaries.

The four walls around a church building do not consist of just brick and mortar. These walls that have divided us are both *inside walls* and *outside walls*. The *inside walls* consist of those things we do to each other such as the pointed finger, petty disagreements, or those old mindsets that have kept us locked into box-like thinking that says, "I'm not sure I want to change." These are walls of fear, rejection, bitterness, insecurity, and walls of the past that we have allowed to dictate our present and our future. These walls grow into cliques and cliques into factions and factions into splits.

Then there are the *outside walls* that have divided us from other churches. These are walls such as the jealousies we have formed, the prejudices we have held, the denominational lines we have drawn, competition between each other and that independent spirit that says, "We don't need you. We can make it on our own." All of this has brought much confusion to communities that are already confused and in desperate need of unity and peace. We see that with all its pain and brokenness. Look upon their faces, gaze into their eyes. There is a silent cry of desperation. Here we experience the reality of a culture without hope. Our call is to become a church without walls, that extension of God's love to a mass of humanity in desperate need of a savior. It is time for the church to rise above the things that have separated us, roll up its sleeves, grab a towel and a bowl of water and go to work. Our call is to be bridges into the hearts of real people that we meet everyday. For God has chosen the church to meet the social needs of the community, to be that redemptive power in our cities.

> *Our call is to be those bridges*
> *into the hearts of real people.*

If every church would do their God-given responsibility, the economy of our nation would be revolutionized. It would fill relational voids, raise the confidence of otherwise destitute individuals and help millions of people use their God-given abilities to contribute to society. This is not about a hand out; it is all about a hand up.

When the church takes this responsibility, there is a releasing of God's power through His people. It is the power of love coupled with the anointing of God that breaks the old mindsets of poverty, and breaks the attitude, belief and cycle of generational welfare. "Because my mama and daddy have been on welfare and their parents before them, I need to be." No, you don't need to be. God has said, "You are wonderfully and fearfully made, and I am setting you free from that kind of thinking. You are special. You are valuable. You are worth something, and you can get a job, for I have given you My power to succeed."

Whole families will be set free from the curse of poverty all because somebody reached out with a loaf of bread, the anointing was released, and the power of love was shown. This is what the power of love did in one of our local churches. A couple was struggling financially and had already filed for divorce. Somebody in the church gave them a box of food and continued to do this for a few weeks. Out of desperation, they both decided they would check out the church that was giving out something instead of asking for something. By the end of the service, they were holding hands and asked the pastor to help them put their marriage back together. They made a decision to drop the divorce papers. Somebody was obedient, somebody cared and reached out with a loaf of bread.

The church without walls is the answer!

You see, when Jesus fed those 5,000 and the 4,000, something special took place. We say, "Well, it was the miracle of multiplication when God multiplied the bread." But there was something else that took place that day. God was using that food, that expression of love by Jesus, to break off old ways of thinking, breaking down walls of indifference. Yes, the power of love prepared their hearts to receive the teaching. When you have single moms trying to make a decision whether to clothe their children or pay the light bill or eat, and somebody comes along with a box of food — that is a miracle. This anointing of God, this power of love, and this miracle will change a life and transform a community — all because the church reached out with that loaf of bread.

When this love that is in us is visibly seen and expressed by others, the walls come down, independent spirits are broken off, competition is destroyed, Satan's accusations are thwarted and lost souls begin to seek this love that is so misunderstood and foreign to the world. Just as water flows through a conduit, the anointing is in every believer as I John 2:27 reads, *"But the anointing which you have received from Him abides in you."* This anointing is released through us to meet others in their need, thereby breaking off social and economic strongholds and addictions, reconciling families, and bringing transformation to communities.

Is the church prepared to step up to the plate in social services? Martin Luther King wrote in his book, *Strength To Love*, "The Christian gospel is a two-way road. On the one hand, it seeks to change the souls of men and thereby unite them with God; on the other hand, it seeks to change the environmental conditions of man so that the soul will have a chance after it is changed. Any religion that professes to be concerned with the souls of men and is not concerned with the slums that damn them, the economic conditions that strangle them, and the social conditions that cripple them is a dry-as-dust religion."[1]

By and large, the church is not prepared. We have relegated our God-given responsibility to the government. The people living in our communities should be able to come to the church for their help and their answers. But how is the church going to help them with their physical needs if the church is still hung up with its own needs? How are they going to get help with their racial issues if the church is hung up culturally?

One day a friend phoned me and told me that the Lord had blessed their church with total revival through their food ministry. He went on to share the miracles the Lord had done, which included restoration of families in their church and unity among churches of other denominations. He further said, "Our church was once a dead, unmotivated church and is now revived and reaching out to the community."

The church needs to be set free of the walls that have divided us from one another – walls of indifference, fear, jealousy, legalism, competition, and prejudice. When clergy and public officials speak of the need to lower the crime rate in a particular community, we need to look at what will make a difference. What will break the yokes of violence and oppression off an entire community, set people free of addictions, break the bondage of unforgiveness, hate and bitterness, break the yoke of prejudice, the yoke of greed and immorality, and the drive for power? What is it that will reconcile marriages, bring the prodigals home and radically change a community? The answer: *Obedience to the call, the mandate of Isaiah 58, resulting in a greater releasing of the anointing.*

The church without walls is also a church that recognizes that the business owners and business leaders of their church are a great resource, both with their finances and their employees, in meeting the needs of the less fortunate. These businesses represent an untapped resource of skills that can be used to reach out beyond the walls of the corporate world to bring healing, restoration and hope to those in need. The church without walls recognizes that the Mandate of Isaiah 58 — *"to divide your bread with the hungry and bring the homeless poor into the house and when you see the naked to clothe them"* — is that they should challenge their business leaders to be involved in and not deny them the opportunity to receive blessings to their businesses.

God only knows how many businesses need their healing to spring forth quickly: healing of employee/employer relationships, and healing within the employees' families, both physically and emotionally. Businesses also need the glory of the Lord to be their rear guard, protecting their business and employees from the attacks of the enemy and from his one objective — to steal, kill, and destroy. Businesses would become like well-watered gardens, prospering in all that they do. As a result of their reaching out to their communities by using their skills and financial resources, they will become known as rebuilders of the waste places of their communities, repairers of the breaches in peoples' lives, and restorers of the neighborhoods where they dwell. The church without walls recognizes that it is time to step up to the plate by challenging every business owner and business leader to open their eyes to the communities around them, and, as they look to the crowds, their hearts will break and they will begin to give back to the communities that serve them.

PREFACE

*"And let us consider one another in order to stir up
love and good works, not forsaking the assembling
of ourselves together, as is the manner of some, but
exhorting one another, and so much the more
as you see the Day approaching."*
Hebrews 10:24-25

I believe that God wants to stir us up and that we will never
be the same after reading this book. I believe we are about
to go to a whole new level in our lives. We will experience
a level of ministry that, perhaps, we have never experienced
before. We will witness the reality of God incarnate (Jesus
come in the flesh) as we give that drink of water to the thirsty
and that touch of compassion to the wounded. I believe in
miracles, and I believe that God wants to do a miracle in our
lives, in our churches, in our businesses, and in our communities. Perhaps some of us, as leaders, are a bit reluctant to
read this book. We're faithful and really want to serve, but
we're not sure of our purpose. We have read so many books

and listened to so many CDs, and yet nothing ever seems to happen. We have tried many things, and we often feel confused and frustrated.

Do you need a breakthrough?

Some of us are praying and hoping for a breakthrough. We need a breakthrough in our finances, in our ministries, in our businesses, and in our relationships. We need a breakthrough in our marriage and with our children. We need a breakthrough in our church. Some of us are holding on to the past. We're bitter and miserable. We are trying to put new wine into old wine skins. As long as we keep hanging out in our own selfish world, we will not embrace the destiny that God has for us. God wants to break off those bondages that plague us from our past – unfulfilled dreams, a failed marriage or business, someone who did not treat us fairly, or a ministry that fell short of our expectations. Something in our lives didn't go the way we wanted it to, and we are still hung up with the past. We have to let it go. But now is our time for a breakthrough — to rise to another level. For too long we have been on this confining side. And as Jesus said to His disciples, *"Let us cross over to the other side"* (Mark 4:35), it's time for the church to cross over. Who was waiting on the other side when Jesus and His disciples got out of the boat? It was a man with an unclean spirit. It was a miracle waiting to happen!

Rise up, Church, and heed to the call

"Is this not the fast that I have chosen:
To loose the bonds of wickedness,
To undo the heavy burdens,
To let the oppressed go free,
And that you break every yoke?

Is it not to share your bread with the hungry,
And that you bring to your house
the poor who are cast out;
When you see the naked, that you cover him,
And not hide yourself from your own flesh?

Then your light shall break forth like the morning,
Your healing shall spring forth speedily,
And your righteousness shall go before you;
The glory of the LORD shall be your rear guard.

Then you shall call, and the LORD will answer;
You shall cry, and He will say, 'Here I am.'
If you take away the yoke from your midst,
The pointing of the finger, and speaking wickedness,

If you extend your soul to the hungry
And satisfy the afflicted soul,
Then your light shall dawn in the darkness,
And your darkness shall be as the noonday.

The LORD will guide you continually,
And satisfy your soul in drought,
And strengthen your bones;
You shall be like a watered garden,
And like a spring of water, whose waters do not fail.

Those from among you
Shall build the old waste places;
You shall raise up the foundations
of many generations;
And you shall be called the Repairer of the Breach,
The Restorer of Streets to Dwell In."
Isaiah 58:6-12

Isaiah 58 tells us that God's purpose for us is to be rebuilders of the ancient ruins, to raise up the age-old foundations, and to be called repairers of the breach and restorers of the streets in which we dwell. I like the *Message Bible* version of Isaiah 58:12, *"You'll use the old rubble of past lives to build anew, rebuild the foundations from out of your past. You'll be known as those who can fix anything, restore old ruins, rebuild and renovate, make the community livable again."* This was the cry of the prophet, Isaiah, some 700 years before Christ. This same cry has echoed through the halls of time, a cry that the church would rise up to its call. Another cry echoes through those halls of time. It is the voice of Nehemiah. For when he heard that the people of his childhood city were in great distress, and the walls of the city were broken down and its gates were burned with fire, the Bible says, *"So it was, when I heard these words, that I sat down and wept, and mourned for many days; I was fasting and praying before the God of heaven"* (Nehemiah 1:4). Nehemiah, however, did not remain in his grief; He rose, praying and fasting, seeking the Lord's guidance. Then he set in motion what the Lord was showing him to do. His whole purpose was to bring restoration and peace into that city. The people had a mind to work, and when the critics came along and opposition arose, Nehemiah's response was, *"...I am doing a great work, so that I cannot come down..."* (Nehemiah 6:3).

We have the awesome privilege and responsibility to serve, to divide our bread, to divide our lives and to speak hope, restoration, and forgiveness into other peoples' lives — to be that carrier of restoration and conduit of healing. Walk along the streets in your community. Look upon the people in your neighborhoods, see the waste places and meet the battered, broken, and confused. Listen behind those doors to what is going on in many families. "Well, we haven't gotten along in years. Everybody is better off since we got a divorce." "You bet I'm concerned about my kids, but I also need to think about me for once. They'll make it." The family is in crisis today. See the waste places of your communities. Ruth Foster of Westwood Assembly of God in White Center, Seattle, Washington, shared the following testimony with me. "Loren was homeless for many years, living on the streets, using drugs and alcohol as the way to exist. He had broken bones from the many beatings he had experienced, and had trouble with his speech because of the drugs he had taken. After coming to church for clothes and food for over two years, he accepted the Lord and now has an apartment and a home church. God has worked miracles in his life. He is now sober, healthier, and thanking God. He still comes to visit us once a month to thank us for caring for him."

There is good news! Our God reigns! This is why we're here on this earth. God is still in the business of reclaiming whole communities and their people. This is our purpose.

Why don't we see more miracles and more power when we look at our churches today? Why don't we see the power of God to the extent that the apostles did in the Book of Acts? Why are we still running to the altar with the same problems, the same struggles? Why are we just over broke most of the time? And why do so few Christians have a purpose in their lives?

A young woman from a local church took some food to a needy family in an apartment house in Redmond, Washington. The husband was reluctant to accept the food but told his wife that she could take it. He needed to get to a job interview, went out to start his car, and it wouldn't start. He went back into the house, angry, telling his wife, "See, I can't even get to my job interview." The young woman who brought the food said, "I'll take you." He replied, "Why would you take me?" She replied, "Because of Jesus' love." He consented, they got down the street a ways, and he asked, "Would you pull into that store? I need some cigarettes." So she did, and he went in to buy his cigarettes. The first thing he said when he got back into the car was, "Why didn't you judge me for smoking?" She replied, "Because of Jesus' love." He went to his interview and then returned home. Two days later, the woman called the young Christian girl and said, "My husband wants to talk to you." She went to their home, and the first words out of his mouth were, "Would you tell me about this Jesus' love? I don't understand." After she explained Jesus to the man, sharing the good news of the gospel, he received Christ right in his living room.

God did not intend the work of the ministry to be confined within the four walls of the church. But, rather, the church would primarily consist of an equipping center where each person is trained, built up and encouraged in the Word and then released to do the work of the ministry in the community. Therefore Isaiah 58 becomes a vehicle for ministry by which we become bridges into peoples' hearts, much like a channel or conduit. As water flows through a conduit, so the anointing flows through us. Isaiah 58 then becomes a reality when every yoke is broken, families are restored, marriages are reconciled, churches are revived and whole communities are transformed. This is really about the WHAT of Ministry and when you have the WHAT in place, then you will have transformation.

Isaiah 58 becomes a vehicle for ministry

CHAPTER ONE

TUNE INTO GOD

Is this not the fast that I have chosen...
Isaiah 58:6

"*I*s this not the fast that I have chosen..." The key words here are "I have chosen." This is all about Him. This is what God wants. His will. His way. This is what we need to be about. The Hebrew word for "chosen" is *bachar*, meaning "require." In other words, "Is this not the fast I require?" So, it's all about Him. It starts with God, it ends with Him, and He maintains it.

Before we can become that church without walls, we need God to expose, deal with, and tear down the *inside walls*. Before we can give out, we have to give up and give in. The walls of discord and the pointed finger with which we have shot the wounded, rather than restore them, is a stench in God's nostrils. He sees the competition and pride of owner-ship, and I believe He weeps for those who cannot praise Him because they cannot see Him in His body. Attitudes and mindsets will need to change. We will need to bring to the cross prejudices we have held, religious traditions that have kept us in bondage and petty attitudes that have resulted in cliques, factions and splits. To do this we will first need to get tuned into Him.

> *"...Consecrate yourselves, for tomorrow the Lord will do wonders among you."*

When we're trying to tune into our favorite radio station, and we're not quite on the right frequency, we get all kinds of static and interference. Perhaps we have experienced that in ministry. Is it any wonder why we feel frustrated and burned out? Joshua 3:5 says, *"..."Sanctify yourselves, for tomorrow the LORD will do wonders among you."* We want to take our cities for the kingdom, but first we need to take our own souls. In II Chronicles 29, King Hezekiah has just gathered together the priests and the Levites, saying to them in verse 5, *"Hear me, Levites! Now sanctify yourselves, sanctify the house of the LORD God of your fathers, and carry out the rubbish from the holy place."* What is unclean in the church today starts with the individual. The bitterness, the finger pointing, the prideful attitudes, the competitive and jealous spirit, and all the division and back biting and power plays all need to be addressed and dealt with.

James 1:9 says in the New Living Translation, *"Christians who are poor should be glad, for God has honored them."* How does He honor the poor? I believe that Psalm 22:24 tells us that He honors the poor in two ways. First of all, He does not ignore their need, their suffering. Verse 24 says, *"For He has not despised nor abhorred the affliction of the afflicted; Nor has He hidden His face from Him; But when*

He cried to Him, He heard." Secondly, He has listened to their cry for help. God has seen their need, their suffering, and He has heard their prayers for help. I believe at this point He answers their prayers for help through the church. This is really about God's people responding to His Word in Isaiah 58:7, *"Is it not to share your bread with the hungry, And that you bring to your house the poor who are cast out; When you see the naked, that you cover him, And not hide yourself from your own flesh?"* So it behooves us, the church, to hear those cries for help. We have to be tuned into God because I believe He puts those cries into our spirit and into our soul — our mind, will and emotions. Then we are ready to act upon what we have heard. God told one of my sons to give some money to a person who was sitting just two rows in front of him at church. Out of obedience, he handed this person some money after the service and said, "God told me you needed this." It turned out to be the exact amount she needed to pay the rest of her rent. God told him this in his spirit, it was translated to his soul and he acted upon it. But what happens so much of the time is that our soul gets so clouded with our own selfish ways that we miss what God is asking us to do — to meet the needs of the afflicted.

Prayer Focus: "Dear God, search me and try me and expose those *inside walls* that have kept me in bondage to myself. Forgive me for the way I have treated those you have forgiven. Cleanse me of my selfish attitudes and my pointed finger that has been so quick to criticize. Cleanse me, oh God, of my prejudices. Father, I ask you to put a guard over my heart, my thoughts, and my mind. I commit my life anew to you. I want you on the throne of my life. Your kingdom come and your will be done. In Jesus' name."

Ecclesiastes 3:11 says, *"...He has put eternity in their hearts."* What is the Holy Spirit saying? He has given us an eternal perspective toward life so that we will look beyond the routines, circumstances, prejudices, and competition. We must get beyond the usual, beyond the humdrum. We need to ask ourselves, "What is going to make an eternal difference? What are the things that are going to matter for all eternity?"

The man or woman who is tuned into God will have an eternal perspective toward his or her own life. What things in our lives are really going to matter for all eternity? What is really important versus urgent? There are a lot of things that are urgent, but only a few that are important.

Clean up what's on the inside

I will sing of mercy and justice;
To You, O LORD, I will sing praises.
I will behave wisely in a perfect way.
Oh, when will You come to me?
I will walk within my house with a perfect heart.
I will set nothing wicked before my eyes;
I hate the work of those who fall away;
It shall not cling to me.
A perverse heart shall depart from me;
I will not know wickedness.
Whoever secretly slanders his neighbor,
Him I will destroy;
The one who has a haughty look and a proud heart,
Him I will not endure.
My eyes shall be on the faithful of the land,

That they may dwell with me;
He who walks in a perfect way,
He shall serve me.
He who works deceit shall not
dwell within my house;
He who tells lies shall not continue in my presence.
Early I will destroy all the wicked of the land,
That I may cut off all the evildoers
from the city of the LORD.
Psalm 101

In Psalm 101, God gives us the qualities of a man and woman of God who are tuned into making an eternal difference in their personal life.

ARE YOU FOCUSED?

"I will sing of mercy and justice; To You, O LORD, I will sing praises" (Psalm 101:1). We will look for You, seek You, give our full attention to You, and we will worship You. Our whole focus is to be tuned into God.

Much of the time our gaze and glance are mixed up. An unkind word, a stressful phone call we were not expecting, a bill in the mail we thought we had paid, that deal we thought was going through but failed. All this in the course of a day's time, and our whole focus becomes consumed with our circumstances. Contrast this with putting our gaze upon the Lord and our glance on our circumstances. Then He is magnified and our circumstances are diminished in His greatness.

In Psalm 34:10, we read, *"The young lions lack and suffer hunger; But those who seek the LORD shall not lack any good thing."* In Psalm 27:8, the Lord commands us to seek His face, *"When You said, 'Seek My face,' My heart said to You, 'Your face, LORD, I will seek.'"* Psalm 105:4 says, *"Seek the LORD and His strength; Seek His face evermore!"* And in Psalm 17:15, the Living Bible reads, *"But as for me, my contentment is not in wealth but in seeing you and knowing all is well between us. And when I awake in Heaven, I will be fully satisfied, for I will see you face to face."* Isn't that awesome? Our relationship with our Heavenly Father should really turn us on and give us contentment.

Be a God seeker

To help us get squared away in our focus, we need to be first of all a God seeker.

"My soul, wait silently for God alone,
For my expectation is from Him.
He only is my rock and my salvation;
He is my defense;
I shall not be moved.
In God is my salvation and my glory;
The rock of my strength,
And my refuge, is in God.
Trust in Him at all times, you people;
Pour out your heart before Him;
God is a refuge for us. Selah"
Psalm 62:5-8

Right Perspective

When we come under His kingdom authority it is about having right perspective. The perspective that we have toward our earthly father will often affect our view toward our Heavenly Father. So much of the time today, many people have a distorted view of Father God. We mention "Father" and many folks relate to Him the way they related to or didn't relate to their earthly dad. If dad was a yeller and an angry, domineering, manipulative or abusive man, we probably see God as domineering, demanding, and manipulative. If dad was a man of compassion, then we see God as gentle, loving, and caring.

I spoke with a man a few years back after I had just finished participating in his dad's funeral. "Tell me about your dad," I asked. He told me his dad was strong, honest, and very caring. This brought to mind my own dad, who loved my mom deeply and was a lover of people. He was also an encourager and a supporter. One thing that stands out for me is that I can never remember a time my dad was not there for me. Even though he was a very busy man, he was always up in the stands of life, cheering me on. He would yell, "That's my son down there! Do you see him? He's over there. Yes, sir, that's my son." That was my dad, the kind of hero that every young man needs. And that is the way I view my Heavenly Father. He is my Hero and my Cheerleader!

What is our Heavenly Father really like?

We need to know our Heavenly Father. We need to learn the character of God. What is He really like? The Bible tells us about His character. *"He only is my rock and my salvation; He is my defense; I shall not be moved. In God is my salvation and my glory; the rock of my strength, And my refuge, is in God."* (Psalm 62:6-7). The Bible tells us that He's our Provider when the middle of the month comes, and we have bills to pay and no money to pay them. *"And my God shall supply all your need according to His riches in glory by Christ Jesus."* (Philippians 4:19). And when we think we've come to a place where everybody has deserted us, He's there. *"I will never leave you or forsake you"* (Hebrews 13:5). When we know His character, we are more comfortable in trusting and submitting to Him. Submitting is really about the Lord's Prayer. *"Thy Kingdom come, thy will be done in my life, in my relationships, in my home, as it is being done in heaven."* Get really practical with God. "God, I submit my mind to You today."

> *"I beseech you therefore, brethren, by the mercies of God, that you present your bodies a living sacrifice, holy, acceptable to God, which is your reasonable service. And do not be conformed to this world, but be transformed by the renewing of your mind, that you may prove what is that good and acceptable and perfect will of God."*
> *Romans 12:1-2*

The perfect will of God for us is to have a transformed, renewed mind. To do this, we need to think of those things that are pure, right, lovely, just, honorable, and worthy of praise. What this is really all about is worship, and worship is a condition of the heart. "I love the Lord my God with all my heart, soul, and mind." The eyes of the Lord are running to and fro searching for a heart that is completely fixed on Him. *"For as he thinks in his heart, so is he"* (Proverbs 23:7). How is your heart?

Prayer Focus: "All right, Lord, it's just You and me, and You know the real me. No one else does, so help me now to take You at your word, one step at a time. Let there be a building of consistency in my life. Let me reflect You and not try to project You upon the people I encounter today. Wash me in Your blood and empower me with a clear conscience, that I may be the leader that You want me to be, in Jesus Name."

Let me reflect You and not try to project You...

The enemy wants to stop us from making any kind of progress in focusing on our Heavenly Father. He wants to keep us in a life of sin and defeat. It is all about focus at the point of temptation. "Lord, it is You I need when I am tempted. It is you, Father, that will deliver me." It all boils down to focus.

I love Snicker Bars. We are usually tempted with something we really like. The point is this: When there are the "Snicker Bars" of life, God doesn't want us to go for the Snicker Bars. He wants us to decide that obeying Him is more important than the taste of the Snicker Bar, and focus will turn our thoughts from the Snicker Bar to the Father.

Take Action: Where are we with the Snicker Bars in our lives? Commit to praying something like this: "Lord, keep me today from anything I can't handle. Keep me from anything today that would cause me to stumble and embarrass You. Keep Your promise in my life that You gave me in 1 Corinthians 10:13, *"No temptation has overtaken you except such as is common to man; but God is faithful, who will not allow you to be tempted beyond what you are able, but with the temptation will also make the way of escape, that you may be able to bear it."*

DO YOU HAVE RIGHT PRIORITIES?

"I will behave wisely in a perfect way.
Oh, when will You come to me?"
Psalm 101:2

There are many things that are urgent. They are good, well meaning things. But only a few are important. We need to learn to distinguish between what is urgent and what is important.

It is early in the morning, and we have just sat down to read the Word and pray, and we remember that we were supposed to call someone. To make that call is a well-meaning thing, and I am sure very necessary, but it is not the most important thing at the moment. It is one of those urgent things that we need to do later. It is about that close walk with the Father all week long that will result in successful relationships.

Distinguish between what is urgent
and what is important

In Matthew 21:13, Jesus talks about cleansing the temple. He said, *"'My house shall be called a house of prayer,' but you have made it a 'den of thieves.'"* We have done that to the Lord's temple — our own bodies. We have concerned ourselves with everything else but our intimacy with the Father. We need to be sure that we have taken care of His person, that we have His plan, His Kingdom, and His glory in order.

In my Father's lap...

When my children were small, I would come home from work, and they would always be there to meet me at the door, saying, "Daddy, daddy, daddy." I can remember the many times they would climb into my lap and seem perfectly content because they were in their daddy's lap. That is what we need to be — perfectly content sitting in our Father's lap, focusing on our Father. In our Father's lap there is rest. In our Father's lap there is security and protection. Psalm 91:7 says, *"A thousand may fall at your side, and ten thousand at your right hand; but it shall not come near you."* In our Father's lap there is healing and hope that today will be better than yesterday. In our Father's lap there is love with no strings attached, no conditions. Our Father just loves us, and there is nothing that we can do that will make our Daddy love us any less or any more. He just loves us and keeps on loving us.

A lady in one of my former ministries wrote this poem, which describes the love of the Father so well.

Rock-a-bye sweet child,
Let my love be your lullaby.
I understand your tender heart
And I hear you when you cry.
I am moved by your loneliness
And I have seen your fear.
I love You, you are my child
And I am very near.

I understand your deepest thoughts,
I know them everyone.
I wanted you to have new joy
So I gave you my Son.

Oh, let go and I will be your Father
With pure and perfect love.
I will not hurt you, you can trust me,
I am gentle as a dove.

And I long to put the dance of joy
Back into your soul.
I will renew your tired heart
And make what's broken, whole.

So Rock-a-bye sweet child,
Let my love be your lullaby.
I understand your tender heart
I hear you when you cry.

Before we can hope to have a right perspective toward anything in life, we must have the right view of God. He loves us and is not an abuser but a forgiver. He doesn't hold things against us. We can trust Him. He is very secure, and because of that we can be confident in Him. He wants to be Daddy, Abba Father, to us. That is what fathers want. He doesn't want to be a stranger to us; He wants to be personal. This reflects total dependency on Him. "Father, I need you. I'm in this big world out here, and I feel so lonely. I don't know what to do. Dad, I need you."

Fatherhood also speaks of obedience. In other words, to be Dad means to be the final word. You see, if He is Dad, He wants to be near, but He also wants to be in charge. So many times we come to God and tell Him what to do. We try to tell God what we are going to do today and ask Him to bless it. But dads don't operate that way. So many of our problems are a result of not having right priorities and losing perspective. Our problems magnify, and pressures get worse because we're trying to do everything in our own strength. It has been said that He should be our best friend because He loves us, and we should bow at His feet because He exercises that love out of Heaven. In other words, "I am your friend, but I am also your Father. You can play and have a great time, but you must obey and respect me."

Take Action: Write down those changes that you must make to have right priorities and then determine through prayer that you will change. Remember, as the late Edwin Louis Cole put it so aptly: "Change is not change until we change."

DO YOU MAKE A COVENANT WITH YOUR EYES?

"I will set nothing wicked before my eyes.
"Psalm 101:3

Men, this area should take high priority in our lives because, as men, we are primarily visual. What we see is what affects us in our mind, thoughts, will, emotions, and physical body. It will also affect our marriages. So pay careful attention to what you focus your eyes upon. Matthew 6:22-23 says, *"The lamp of the body is the eye. If therefore your eye is good, your whole body will be full of light. But if your eye is bad, your whole body will be full of darkness. If therefore the light that is in you is darkness, how great is that darkness!"* When our eyes become clouded with the things of this world, our whole life is affected. This is why when a man is looking with lust in his heart upon another woman, it will eventually affect his whole body and his marriage. Genesis 2:24 says, *"Therefore a man shall leave his father and mother and be joined to his wife, and they shall become one flesh."* When a man lusts after another woman, he brings darkness not only on his own body but also his wife's body.

What do you focus on? What kind of books or magazines do you read? What movies and TV programs do you watch? In many of our homes, we have set a double standard. We have asked our children to do one thing while we turn around and do that very thing we say we don't approve of. We have become pros at rationalizing our position by saying things like, "Well, they're just not mature enough yet." Consider this as food for thought. If it's not good enough for our children, is it really good enough for us? Much of the temptation that we are confronted with is either eliminated or embraced when we choose to turn away with our eyes or choose to look upon it. I have often counseled men who struggle with lust to avoid the magazine racks when they go into a market. The Bible says, *"I have made a covenant with my eyes"* (Job 31:1).

Take Action: Do you have control of your eyes, or do your eyes have control of you? Verbally make a commitment to the Holy Spirit by asking Him to control your eyes. Then take the initiative to turn away from those things that tempt you.

HAVE YOU HAD YOUR HEART CHECKED LATELY?

"A perverse heart shall depart from me;
I will not know wickedness."
Psalm 101:4

The Bible says in Proverbs 23:7, *"For as he thinks in his heart, so is he."* We spend a lot of time strengthening our physical heart with exercise and right nutrition, but what about our spiritual heart? First of all, we need to be concerned about having a clean heart. Psalm 51:10 says, *"Create in me a clean heart, O God."* In the Lord's Prayer are these words: *"Your kingdom come. Your will be done on earth as it is in heaven"* (Matthew 6:10). To bring this home, we might read it this way: "Your Kingdom come into my life, Your will be done in my life as it is being done in Heaven." I wonder when we pray these words if we understand their significance. There is no selfishness or bitterness in the Lord's Heaven. There is no fight for rights in the Lord's Heaven. Is anyone broke in Heaven? No. Is anyone sick in Heaven? No. Is anyone getting a divorce in Heaven? No. Then God doesn't want these things down here for us either.

When we are sincere about knowing and doing the Lord's will, our hearts will change, and we will experience major attitude adjustments. It's like peeling an onion a layer at a time. When we want the Lord to establish His Kingdom, His will in our life, in our marriage, in our job, in our businesses, in our finances, and in our health, then the Father begins to work His practical righteousness into our lives. He starts to expose, and dispose of, those impurities and those toxic attitudes such as greed and self-centeredness. He eradicates and purges wrong motives and unforgiving attitudes.

In different parts of the country during the fall, the leaves on many trees begin to turn different shades of color and eventually fall off the trees. If we happen to be one of those lucky people who have those kinds of changing trees in our yard, we end up raking the dead leaves. There is a process that causes the leaves to fall off the trees. When fall arrives, the sap from the tree works its way out to the end of the branches and forms a tiny bud. As that bud grows, it pushes the leaf off the tree. So instead of leaves just falling off, they are pushed off. Then in the spring, that tiny bud becomes a beautiful flower, which in turn becomes a beautiful new leaf. You see, we do not pick leaves off the trees. We just let them get pushed off.

Stop picking the leaves

We do the same with our lives. We don't get anxious and try to pick all the sins out of our lives. Like the sap, we get filled up with the presence of God, and He pushes those undesirable things out of our lives so our new beginnings can bloom. We will experience a changed heart because our Father's Kingdom will not share simultaneously with the kingdom of this world. We can't consistently ask the Father to establish His Kingdom in our lives and not experience a dramatic change of heart.

We need to have a joyful heart. Proverbs 17:22 says, *"A merry heart does good, like medicine."* Good medicine leads to good healing. Have you ever noticed how many grumpy looking Christians there are? They look like they have just lost their best friend. Read this carefully: If you are one of those grumpy Christians, your mind and your heart are probably out of whack from the world's way of thinking — focusing on television, reading unwholesome books, or constantly listening to negative conversations. Oftentimes there can be a bad spirit associated with some of that stuff, and it just wants to get all over you. Shake it off. Get rid of it. Be careful. Get a grip. Proverbs 15:13 says, *"A merry heart makes a cheerful countenance, but by sorrow of the heart the spirit is broken."* When we have a joyful heart, it's contagious. People can see it, and they are drawn to us.

We need to be sure that our hearts are contrite and humble. Psalm 51:17 says, *"A broken and a contrite heart— These, O God, You will not despise."* Then there's James 4:6, *"God resists the proud, but gives grace to the humble."* And Philippians 2:3-4 tells us to *"Let nothing be done through*

47

selfish ambition or conceit, but in lowliness of mind let each esteem others better than himself. Let each of you look out not only for his own interests, but also for the interests of others." This rubs against the grain of our natural man. We don't naturally regard others more important than ourselves and look to their interests. So how do we know that? Well, how's it going with your driving lately? Someone needs to get in, and you've already been waiting. You know that light because you drive through the same intersection every day. It only lets so many cars through, and if you let that guy in, it's a good chance you'll miss the light. Of course, you're thinking, "*I* might be late to work."

How about this one? I love steak with the bone in it because I like to chew on the bone. When my kids were growing up, they all liked the bone, too. One day I was given the only steak with the bone. Do you think I humbled myself enough to share that bone? As we check out our heart, we not only need to be concerned about a clean, joyful, and humble heart, but we need to take a look at the motives of our serving. The Bible teaches us to *"Keep your heart with all diligence, for out of it spring the issues of life"* (Proverbs 4:23).

What is it that moves our heart to be pure and leads us to serve others? When Jesus looked at the crowds, the Bible tells us in Matthew 9:36, *"But when He saw the multitudes, He was moved with compassion for them, because they were weary and scattered, like sheep having no shepherd."* The New Living Translation reads, *"He felt great pity for the crowds that came, because their problems were so great and they didn't know where to go for help. They were like sheep without a shepherd."* When we look on the crowds, are we seeing what Jesus saw? Or have we become so inner-focused on our problems and insulated by our self-centeredness that we feel little or no compassion? Jesus was moved with compassion. But when we look at a man standing on the corner with a sign that reads, "I need help, please help me, God bless you," do we think, "Oh, there's one of those panhandlers," or do we look at that man through the eyes of Jesus? Do we stop to consider what brought this man to the corner? Have we thought that people don't get there overnight? Perhaps it started years before when a tragedy hit his life. Where were we then? Will we pass him instead of being a good Samaritan? No, because it is God's love that compels us to stop, to turn around, and to help. It is God's love that motivates us to serve. The Bible says, *"The love of God has been poured out in our hearts by the Holy Spirit who was given to us"* (Romans 5:5). It is in that love that compassion is born. It is in that love that we are propelled into a mindset that says, "I will serve who you want me to serve." Oh, Church, when was the last time we cried out to the Lord that we felt great pity for the crowd? Crowds, crowds, everywhere people in despair. Problems too great to handle. Don't know what to do, nowhere to turn. I believe the Holy Spirit is saying to the Church, "Enough is enough." We must no longer pass them by on the other side.

Take Action: Check your heart. Ask the Holy Spirit to help you to be diligent in guarding your heart from pride, selfishness, impurity, and discouragement. "Change my heart, O God. Give me a heart that breaks when I see those in need. Break down the walls of prejudice that keep me locked in. I don't want to stay bound behind those walls that I have fabricated, thinking they will keep me safe and secure, only to find that I was really in bondage."

WITH WHOM DO YOU ASSOCIATE?

My eyes shall be on the faithful of the land,
that they may dwell with me;
he who walks in a perfect way, he shall serve me.
Psalm 101:6

Who speaks into your life? This is really all about influence. If we are continually around negative, critical, and doubting people, we will find ourselves taking on a lot of those same characteristics. It has been said that there are two types of people in the world. Some walk through a pasture and see only the beautiful wild flowers; others walk through the pastures of life and see only the buffalo chips. We may be associated right now with people who have an eye for the chips and not the flowers. We need a change of influence. We need to get around positive, faith-filled, encouraging people who speak faith and life into our lives and the lives of those around us. We need to get around people who are visionary and excited about what God is doing.

Take Action: Who are the people you hang with? You may need to make a change. Make a list right now of some positive, faith-building people. Then make a decision to invite them over for dessert or dinner.

ARE YOU A PRAYING PERSON?

"Early I will destroy all the wicked of the land,
that I may cut off
all the evildoers from the city of the LORD."
Psalm 101:8

This is really all about spiritual warfare. II Corinthians 10:5 says, *"For the weapons of our warfare are not carnal but mighty in God for pulling down strongholds, casting down arguments and every high thing that exalts itself against the knowledge of God, bringing every thought into captivity to the obedience of Christ."* In the name of Jesus, and through the blood of Jesus, we have authority over the enemy. I have heard it said that we are most powerful when we are on our knees. My whole prayer life was dramatically changed when I read a book by Larry Lea, entitled *Could You Not Tarry One Hour?* It consisted of a study on the Lord's Prayer — learning to pray the way Jesus would have us pray. I learned how self-centered and need-centered my prayers had been and how I needed to seek the face of God long before I sought His hand. I learned to set my heart upon the Lord — to worship, adore, and honor Him — and to desire His Kingdom to come in my life and His will to be done as it is being done in Heaven. I Timothy 2:8 says, *"I desire therefore that the men pray everywhere, lifting up holy hands, without wrath and doubting."* I believe the Holy Spirit is saying, "I want men who are developing a lifestyle of prayer."

My pastor, Dr. Wendell Smith, Senior Pastor of The City Church in Kirkland, Washington, has said many times, "There are three areas that most men struggle with probably more than anything else: impurity, anger, and unbelief that leads to discouragement. The key to living a life of purity and victory over our habits and struggles is based on prayer. The single most life-changing principle is prayer." We say, "Well, wait a minute. I don't really have an anger or lust problem." Then we likely have another problem: pride. We will not be an overcomer by just trying to do better. We have to pray.

> ### Seek the face of God long before
> ### you seek His hand

YOUR FAMILY LIFE

A second major area where we are to be tuned into God is that we are to make an eternal difference in our home. If we can't lead, don't lead, or won't lead at home, we won't lead out there in the world. Before God can trust us with many people, He wants to trust us with a few. Leaders often put more of their time into ministry while their families are neglected. Shame on them! They lead everyone else in prayer, but what about their family? They have time for everyone else: they call on the sick, counsel the depressed, and so on, but what about their family? Where are you with this matter? You can't truly lead others if you're not willing to lead at home.

> ### Before God can trust us with many people,
> ### He wants to trust us with a few

One day I was driving to the fitness club where I work out and I began to weep. I was overwhelmed with a revelation of how much God loves me. I have experienced His presence and His love for me many times before but never to this depth. In the midst of all this, I heard Him say, "I have shown you this so I can tell you that the practical tangible evidence of My love is the spouse that I have given to you.

Is it any wonder that I have chosen marriage to be an illustration of My Church, for that same love affair that I have with My Bride (the Church) is to be the love affair you have with your bride? This is why I have given to you My Word that husbands are to love their brides as My Son loves His Bride, the Church. And the older women are to teach the younger women how to love their husbands."

The practical application of how all this is to be worked out in our lives is the Song of Solomon. "For in this, I have shown in practical ways the love affair I have with My people and, in application, this is how a man is to love his wife and a wife her husband." It is a love that in practical terms is exciting, passionate and uplifting and filled with affection. This kind of love leaves no room for doubt or insecurity. Solomon speaks to his Bride in chapter 4:9-10, *"You have ravished my heart, my sister, my spouse; you have ravished my heart with one look of your eyes, with one link of your necklace. How fair is your love, my sister, my spouse! How much better than wine is your love, and the scent of your perfumes than all spices!"* The Bride speaks to Solomon in chapter 2:3-4, *"Like an apple tree among the trees of the woods, so is my beloved among the sons. I sat down in his shade with great delight, and his fruit was sweet to my taste. He brought me to the banqueting house, and his banner over me was love."* It is so easy to get all tangled up with the everyday trappings of just living life that we become so focused on the moment and miss the day that He has made. We know that God loves us, but sometimes we need to experience it in a practical way. We need to see that He loves us so much that He demonstrated this love by giving to us our spouses.

Ephesians 5:31-32 says, *"'For this reason a man shall leave his father and mother and be joined to his wife, and the two shall become one flesh.' This is a great mystery, but I speak concerning Christ and the church."* Here He is telling us that the relationship between husband and wife illustrates that which exists between Christ (the Bridegroom) and the Church (His Bride.) In John 17:22-23, Jesus prays for the Church (His Bride): *"And the glory which You gave Me I have given them, that they may be one just as We are one: I in them, and You in Me; that they may be made perfect in one, and that the world may know that You have sent Me, and have loved them as You have loved Me."* When He says, *"I in them, and You in Me,"* I believe He is referring to Himself being in the Church (His Bride) and His Father being in Him. This really sends a message as to the importance of the husband having God in him, having a close intimacy with the Father. He goes on to say, *"that they may be made perfect in one, and that the world may know that You have sent Me, and have loved them as You have loved Me."* This intimacy between one's bride and the Father will result in unity and maturity and will be a beautiful example of God's love to the world. The greatest evangelistic message we have to the world is unified marriage demonstrating the love of God.

Jesus Christ wants to be King of our marriage and our life. Our family life will not get better until Jesus rules in our home. Many Christians give themselves to the work of the flesh then wonder why they don't have peace, righteousness, and joy in their home. Romans 14:17 tells us *"the kingdom of God is not eating and drinking, but righteousness and peace and joy in the Holy Spirit."* In every heart there is a throne and a cross. Christ is on the throne, and self is on the cross. Where we get into trouble is when self is on the throne, and Christ is on the cross. All marriage problems occur when Christ is not ruling one of us in the marriage. The flesh wars against the spirit. The only real resolution for a marital problem is for spouses to bow their knees before God.

It All Hangs on Prayer

Do you want to take confusion, frustration, and fear out of your homes? Then pray, and pray with authority. Husbands, especially, take notice. We need to come to grips with who we are in Christ. *"I can do all things through Christ who strengthens me"* (Philippians 4:13). We need to cut out the "lay me down to sleep" type of praying, and pray with authority. Do not back down to the devil. *"He who is in you is greater than he who is in the world"* (1 John 4:4).

If someone were to break into our homes, rob us, and try to steal our wives and children, would we fight to the death to save them? This is happening in millions of families! Satan is on the prowl, and He is breaking into home after home destroying, stealing, and killing. Divorce among Christians is higher than it has ever been. At a Family Life marriage seminar in April 2002, attendees heard that only one in every 1,017 marriages where couples pray together ended in divorce. However, 500 couples in every 1,017 that did not pray together daily ended in divorce. Staggering, would you agree? Child molestations and kidnappings are more numerous than ever and continuing to shock our society. Men, we have to get serious! Do we really realize how powerful prayer is? I know we say it, we write books about it, we tell others, but what about us in our daily lives? We need to realize that it's about the cross, and focus our attention there. It's because of the cross that we have access to the Heavenly Father.

Hebrews 4:15-16 says, *"For we do not have a High Priest who cannot sympathize with our weaknesses, but was in all points tempted as we are, yet without sin. Let us therefore come boldly to the throne of grace, that we may obtain mercy and find grace to help in time of need."* At the bedside of a sick child, access. When the bills come and there is not enough money, access. When everything around us seems to be caving in, access. In the turbulence of a storm at 40,000 feet, access. At the graveside of a young widow, access. Access to His throne room. Every question answered, every need met, every heart calmed. Access, access.

Husband and wife, pray together — feed your spirits. Praying together can be as intimate as making love to each other. Someone told me once that "intimacy" was sharing all thoughts, feelings, and actions — exposing oneself. Scary, isn't it? We might claim to be soul mates, but our spirit is running on an empty tank. Is it any wonder why we struggle sometimes? Our soul (mind, will, and emotions) is going to revert back to acting out according to the flesh.

> ### *Praying together can be as intimate as making love to each other*

One evening, I was feeling irritated. When my wife made a comment that I did not agree with, I got defensive and ended up saying unkind words to her. By God's grace I recognized what was happening and repented, asking for forgiveness. If I had continued to act like this, it would have eventually led to stress and unhappiness in our marriage. The Song of Solomon 2:15 refers to the little foxes that try to come in and eat at the vineyard — *"Catch us the foxes, the little foxes that spoil the vines, for our vines have tender grapes."* We need to be careful that we guard against the foxes that seek to creep into our relationship.

When we respond to different situations with a fleshly viewpoint, we can become impatient, angry, and unkind. Whereas, when we choose to fill up our spirit with reading the Word and praying in agreement with our spouse, we begin to take on the fruit of the Spirit, which is love, joy, peace, patience, kindness, goodness, faithfulness, and self-control. As we are faced with situations and decisions in the family, we are then able to respond in an uplifting, positive, and encouraging way. Choose to speak life and faith and hope into your families. Focus more on filling up your spirit bank and becoming spirit-mates.

Husbands, if we do not pray with our wives on a consistent daily basis, we are opening our home up to worry and anxiety. By praying together we are setting up a perimeter around our homes. Philippians 4:4-7 tells us to *"Rejoice in the Lord always. Again I will say, rejoice! Let your gentleness be known to all men. The Lord is at hand. Be anxious for nothing, but in everything by prayer and supplication, with thanksgiving, let your requests be made known to God; and the peace of God, which surpasses all understanding, will guard your hearts and minds through Christ Jesus."* Here the Holy Spirit is teaching us that, through prayer, peace will come into our homes and guard our minds and our hearts. Husbands, if we are not experiencing peace in our homes, we need to go to war to fight the good fight of faith and resist the devil.

Pray together daily

Pray together daily. Ecclesiastes 4:9-12 says, *"Two are better than one, because they have a good reward for their labor. For if they fall, one will lift up his companion. But woe to him who is alone when he falls, for he has no one to help him up. Again, if two lie down together they will keep warm; but how can one be warm alone? Though one may be over-powered by another, two can withstand him. And a threefold cord is not quickly broken."* There are many hindrances that keep us from praying together as a couple, including pride and fear. Many men feel inferior to their wives spiritually because society is so performance oriented. This makes it more difficult because we think we have to use eloquent words when we pray, especially as husbands. Wives need to communicate their feelings. Down deep in the recesses of their hearts, almost every woman desires to have a man who will pray with her. Wives, tell your husband your needs. Tell him how you feel and how much you need him to pray with you; but when he does, be careful that you don't criticize him or make yourself look so much more spiritual then he may be.

I recently had a man call me concerning his marriage. I knew that he was a Christian, so I asked if he and his wife prayed together. His answer to me was, "I've been there and tried that, but every time I start to pray with her, she has something critical to offer by telling me that I'm not doing it right. Husbands who constantly hear that just give up." Wives, let me suggest the three P's – praise, patience, and posture. You're probably thinking, "I get it – praise and patience. But what's this posture stuff?" It's your body language. You can send a lot of positive messages by the way you look at him, squeeze his hand, and give him a hug. You're communicating to your husband that he is the man that God put into your life as the spiritual leader, and you're telling him that he is the best. I continually hear those encouraging words from my wife: "John, you are the best!"

Stand watch over your house

In practical terms, we need to pray periodically over the rooms of our house, committing the activities of each room to the Lord. Let's look at a couple of examples. The bedroom is a holy room that we consecrate unto God, a place where God is honored in our communication and in our lovemaking. 1 Corinthians 7 teaches that our bodies are not our own but belong to our spouse and that we are not to deny ourselves from each other, but only for a season of mutual agreement. Lovemaking is not to be used as a tool of manipulation or an attitude that says, "I don't care if my spouse wants to make love; I'm too tired." It is not about you; it's about your spouse and bringing honor to God. The bedroom is to be a place where the spouse is served and ministered to. Ask God for your communication to honor Him and uplift and speak life into your spouse. As for the living room — a place where we entertain — it should glorify God and be known as a place of breakthrough. Make it an oasis of love and understanding, where people are built up and encouraged, where they leave feeling better than when they came.

CHAPTER TWO

BREAK THROUGH AND STOP DWELLING ON THE PAST

"To loose the bonds of wickedness,
to undo the heavy burdens,
to let the oppressed go free."
Isaiah 58:6

Unfulfilled dreams, a marriage that went bad, an employer that was unfair to us, a business that failed, a ministry that fell short of our expectations. In 1 Kings 17, Elijah could have gotten caught up in his circumstances. "Oh, I'm here, Lord, and now look, the brook has dried up. Oh, it's terrible." How many of us have brooks in our lives? T.D. Jakes says, "No storm lasts forever. They come and go, but we choose to live in it forever if we want. Always talking about it and crying about it. The storm leaves us, but we are so caught up talking about it and crying about it, that the storm is raining over our head perpetually."[2]

What am I going to do?

"But Pastor, You don't know what I'm going through." You're right, I don't. But I do know what it is to hear the voice of a doctor tell me my three-year-old son's kidneys will give out, and he will die. I know what it is to have a wife of 26 years leave me for another man. I know what it is to feel the pain and humiliation of financial loss. I know what it is to raise my children flawlessly and see them struggle in their walk and lifestyle. I know what it's like to feel rejection and fear when you lose your job. I know what it is to cry out, "What am I going to do? All the brooks in my life are barren and dried up." I can relate to Elijah. And I can relate to you. We may have a perfect God, but we are living in an imperfect world.

David cried out, *"When my heart is overwhelmed; lead me to the rock that is higher than I"* (Psalm 61:2). We need to come up higher. After all those tests I experienced — weeping at the death bed of my three-year-old son, weeping in my heart over the pregnancy of my unwed daughter, or feeling the pain of a love gone astray — I am here to tell you that there is a God that awaits us and leads us higher.

No matter how dark or long the tunnel we're going through may be, we will make it. God is at work for us. He is a God of turnarounds. He is a God of new beginnings. We can go into His throne room, the throne room for mercy and grace. It's different from the houses of this world — higher than the White House, higher than the courthouse, higher than the feeling of a crack house. When we enter into His house, there is peace and restoration for our souls. When we need more grace to get through our problems, we will receive it. When we need His mercy and His forgiveness because we feel condemnation and guilt, we will receive it. Elijah obeyed God and moved on. We also can deal with our pain and move on.

He is a God of turnarounds

Today all four of my children are serving God. My three-year-old son, whose doctors said was going to die, was miraculously healed; and his life now shows there is a God who is our Deliverer. My daughter is using her mess as a message and her test as a testimony. My middle son is building a business that will help feed many ministries around the world and promote the goodness of the gospel. My oldest son miraculously came through a childhood battle of E. coli to become a man of character and integrity. Even in my own life, God is using the broken pieces of a wounded man to sculpt a masterpiece of hope for others, taking me from ashes to beauty, restoring my life far beyond my wildest dreams and blessing me with Karilyn, my wife, and her daughter and son, and a granddaughter, giving us a blended family of six awesome God-fearing children and ten grandchildren.

When we close the door on the past, we open the door to the future

Elijah obeyed God and moved on. There is a moving on from our past that will liberate us into our destiny. But there are two things that will keep us stuck, that will keep us from moving on: regret of the past and fear of the future.

Paul says, *"...one thing I do, forgetting those things which are behind and reaching forward to those things which are ahead"* (Philippians 3:13). Similarly, Isaiah 43:18-19 tells us, *"Do not call to mind the former things, or ponder things of the past. Behold, I will do something new, now it will spring forth"* (NASB). If we're Christians, our past is under the blood.

"Ponder" according to *Webster's* means "prolonged inclusive thinking about a matter."[3] It implies going over the same matter in our thoughts, again and again. In other words, God is telling us to stop that prolonged thinking of our past, stop bringing it up again and again in our mind, because He wants to do something new. It will spring forth, but we have to quit dwelling on the past so we can begin to see what the "new" is that God is going to bring. Isaiah 44:22 says, *"I have blotted out, like a thick cloud, your transgressions, and like a cloud, your sins. Return to Me, for I have redeemed you."*

Remember the story of Elisha and the widow in 2 Kings 4? Her husband had died, and the creditors were coming to take her two sons to be slaves. Elisha's instructions were that she was to borrow many vessels, go into her house, and shut the door behind her. Twice in these verses, Elisha tells her to shut the door behind her.

I believe there is great significance in shutting the door behind us. I believe the importance of this is that there are doors in our past that need to be shut; in other words, there are certain things that need to be put behind us. There is the door of negative, critical thinking. You were perhaps brought up with the mindset, "You're stupid. You will never amount to anything." All your life you may have been programmed to think you are stupid and anything you try to do will fail. Then there is the door of fear. Every time you have come close to success, it was ripped away from you. And probably the largest door that many folks face is that of bitterness and unforgiveness. Isaiah 58:9 says, *"If you take away the yoke from your midst, the pointing of the finger, and speaking wickedness..."* It has been said that bitterness and unforgiveness are the axes that split up many marriages and hack the hearts out of many a divorcée. We need to take a long hard look in the mirror of life and see where all this leads. It just brings us pain and more pain and causes a whole lot of hurt for others whether they are involved or not. Hebrews 12:15 tells us we should be careful *"lest any root of bitterness springing up cause trouble, and by this many become defiled."* There are some that are stuck in their bitterness, still bitter over former spouses, former employers, or family members. When we shut the door on our past, we open the door to our future and success.

Forgiveness is now

Here is an illustration out of my own life: Before we were married, my wife encouraged me to write a letter to my former spouse and her husband. Karilyn told me that if we were going to have a relationship, I needed to settle the past because it was still haunting me and might cause problems in our marriage. We say, "If I do this and forgive, that person might come back into my life, and I don't want any dealings with him or her." But that's not the issue. The issue is obedience. Emotions run deep through the soul — we feel betrayed, rejected, hurt. Our mind is saying, "I don't want to deal with this, so I'm just going to put it out of my mind." But I'm telling you that God does not say in His Word, "When you get around to feeling it, forgive." He just says, "Forgive." So I wrote my letter out of obedience, not because I felt forgiveness, but because God's Word says in Ephesians 4:32, *"And be kind to one another, tenderhearted, forgiving one another, even as God in Christ forgave you."* I hope that by sharing my letter with you here, it might prompt you to write a similar letter. The names have been changed.

Dear Jill and Jack,

I believe God would want me to write this letter to you and share with you that the Holy Spirit has shown me it is time to write this.

I want to let you know, Jill, that no matter what happened between us, you were and are a great mother to our kids. Our children today would not be all they are for God if you were not the mother you are. You were also a great wife. You gave a lot to our marriage and you kept giving. We had many good years together, and many good memories. I've now come to believe that I want to focus only on those good memories. I can now honestly say that I have been praying for great grace and blessings on your life and marriage to Jack. I no longer hold any bad feelings toward either of you. I believe that is all behind me in the 20th century. I want to go into this 21st century, this new millennium, with nothing but good thoughts and good words toward both of you.

I'm reminded of Isaiah when he says, *"Do not ponder the things of the past, for I'm about to do something new, and it will spring forth speedily."* I also realize that not only is this letter of reconciliation important for you, Jack and me, it is especially important to our children and grandchildren that we can all get along and pray for God's best in each other's lives.

I have come to realize that it takes two to make and break a marriage, and there were things about me that caused stress in your life and ultimately the break up of our marriage. I think everyone blamed you, and my heart grieves that you may have gone through a lot of pain and hurt through all of this, and I ask you to forgive me. I know you heard me say, "I'm sorry" a lot, and perhaps you didn't think I was sincere then, but I hope that you will accept this final "I'm sorry" which comes from the deepest recesses of my heart. I am truly sorry, Jill.

If we did not have children, we could each go our separate ways and never have any contact with each other. But we have three beautiful children who will each have important milestones in their lives — marriage, children, promotions — and many of these momentous occasions will require both of us to be present, most likely with our own spouses. I want those meetings to be memorable for you and me, but more so for our children, grandchildren, and great grandchildren.

Jack, I realize you were blamed for our marriage breakup, but after much heart searching, I've come to realize that if Jill had been totally fulfilled by me, your coming into her life would not have resulted in what happened. So the blame rests equally with me. It is my deepest prayer — I pray every day now for you and Jill — that you will be good to her and that she has found the fulfillment in you that she did not find in me. I want to say to you, from the depths of my heart, that I no longer hold any bitterness or animosity toward you. I forgive you and ask you to forgive me.

How do we get to that point where we are willing to step out in faith and forgive? That person really hurt us, maybe he betrayed us in a way that it hurts every time we think of him. First, we need to seek what Jesus would do. Even after Judas betrayed Jesus, Jesus still called him "friend." How about when Peter sliced off the ear of one of the guards coming to take Jesus? Jesus responded with a healing touch. How can we respond in such a way when we are hurt?

Talk to God. Ask Him to soften your heart. Give Him your resentments and grudges and ask Him to heal your wounds. Begin to pray for that person that hurt you. I know what you're thinking: "It's easy for you to say. You don't know what I've been through." You're right; I don't know your situation. I am not walking in your pain, but the alternative is to keep on hurting. It doesn't take a brain surgeon to know that if we're in pain, and we know the remedy for removing it, we're going to take the steps to do it, right? Well, prayer is definitely the better option; that is, if we want to begin the healing and restoration process. Find someone who is willing to hold you accountable. *"As iron sharpens iron, so a man sharpens the countenance of his friend"* (Proverbs 27:17). We need encouragement and prodding at times like this.

After I wrote my letter, something broke in the Heavens, and I actually felt forgiveness toward my former spouse and her husband. It has been said that when we step up and forgive someone who has offended us, even though she or he doesn't deserve it, we're stepping into God's grace, and God's grace is someplace Satan cannot go.

> *...we're stepping into God's grace, and God's grace is someplace Satan cannot go*

I read the letter to my children before I mailed it, and something miraculous began to happen in the supernatural. Almost immediately they all developed a new attitude toward their mother. When we forgive, we break the stronghold of bitterness. My children were released to forgive their mother. They no longer needed to take up an offense on my part. We are told in 2 Corinthians 10:4-6, *"For the weapons of our warfare are not carnal but mighty in God for pulling down strongholds, casting down arguments and every high thing that exalts itself against the knowledge of God, bringing every thought into captivity to the obedience of Christ, and being ready to punish all disobedience when your obedience is fulfilled."* In other words, it's up to us to make the decision to break a stronghold, and the biggest stronghold that the devil has on an individual today is the stronghold of bitterness. It's up to us to make the choice.

That letter not only affected my children with their mother, but a whole chain of events took place. One evening, we were having dinner with friends, and I began to share what God was doing in my life with my former spouse and her husband. I told them about the letter I had written and what had happened with my children. Suddenly, the woman began weeping. I asked her if I had said something to hurt her, and she responded, "No, I'm all right. I really needed to hear this tonight. I have been very bitter toward my former spouse. Every time I hear his name, I just want to be rid of him. It's just awful, and it's even affected my second marriage and my relationship with my children. I know God is telling me that I need to get over this. Will you and Karilyn help me?"

We suggested that she write a similar letter to her former spouse, and gave her a copy of my letter. She went home and wrote her own letter out of obedience, not feeling it. Three days later she called us and wanted us to read the letter and pray over it with her before she sent it. Two weeks later she called us, crying, and said, "I read the letter to my children, and they read it to their spouses. God is doing a miracle between the kids and me. My former husband also wrote me, forgiving me, and asked for my forgiveness." What an incredible testimony of the power of the cross! You see, she removed that stronghold from her life by punishing disobedience with obedience. Even though she didn't feel forgiveness, she just did it. We can do it, too. No one else can do it for us.

R.J. took my letter, made some changes to make it applicable to his situation, and emailed it to his former spouse, asking her to forgive him. They have a daughter and a grandson; so much was at stake. She replied, "Thank you for your letter. It was a letter of grace. I've received it, not only as a gift of forgiveness from you, but also from God. I feel that now I can move forward and close the door on my past. It is my hope that we can be one of those rare parents that, though they are divorced, can support one another and their children as they move through life. I feel that you've given us that opportunity. Thank you again for blessing me with your letter. It was sunlight to my heart." A few days later, they met for the first time in five years when R.J. delivered their grandson to her for a visit.

Many Christians are stuck in their circumstances and their past. One afternoon, my two-year-old great nephew, Max, said something sarcastic to me while he was playing. His mother heard him and took him off to his room. When he returned, Max said to me, "Uncle John, I am very sorry. Will you forgive me?" My wife told me that he had some help from his mother. That's right. And you and I have help from our parent, our Heavenly Father. He not only tells us what to do but how to do it and what to say. The real difference is that Max was obedient. What about us? *"If you take away the yoke from your midst, the pointing of the finger, and speaking wickedness"* (Isaiah 58:9). It has been said that we punish disobedience with obedience. Start speaking life into others — speak love, speak unity.

A young couple came to see me for some premarital counseling. I asked if there was any bitterness or unforgiveness toward their former spouses. The young woman told me that she had already dealt with those issues and the pain of bitterness. But it became very obvious that the man was still very bitter toward his former spouse. He still had some unresolved issues concerning his former marriage, especially in the area of unforgiveness. I began to share the power of forgiveness with him. I read Matthew 18 and illustrated it in a drawing. This may have been your journey, or perhaps this is where you are right now. I drew a large window with bars and two stick figures behind the bars. One was the man, and the other was his former wife. I placed His fiancée outside the bars where she was free, but he was in prison with his former wife. I asked him if he wanted to be with his former wife in prison or out of prison with his fiancée. Of course, he replied, "I want to be with my fiancée." You see, by his unforgiveness he had not only put himself into bondage, but he had also done the same with his former spouse.

By being willing to respond in faith to what God says, he was set free. Again, Ephesians 4:32 says, *"And be kind to one another, tenderhearted, forgiving one another, even as God in Christ forgave you."* We don't have to feel it. I know what some of you might be thinking: "I don't want to be a hypocrite." Forget about that for now. Just do it because God tells you to do it. In time you will begin to feel it. I can say that because I have been there. I have walked in those same shoes with unforgiveness, bitterness, and even hate in my heart.

So, again, why do we forgive? What are some really gut wrenching reasons? First of all, we forgive because God tells us to forgive. He says, *"...forgiving one another, even as God in Christ forgave you."* (Ephesians 4:32). He says, *"Therefore if you bring your gift to the altar, and there remember that your brother has something against you, leave your gift there before the altar, and go your way. First be reconciled to your brother, and then come and offer your gift."* (Matthew 5:23-24).

Secondly, we forgive because it's really the best for us and the other person. Getting even and harboring bitterness only makes us feel worse. Even if we cause the person who hurt us the worst pain we can inflict, we still don't feel any better because of it. Yes, maybe we think, "Oh, yea, a little bit of revenge..." but guess what? There is no lasting joy in it. Let me remind you that every person who hurts, no matter how deep the hurt, goes through different stages. We first dwell on the thing that made us feel bad, then we go through a "feel sorry for me" stage, and then we want to get even. Our thoughts say, "They really hurt me. I wish some really bad things would happen to them. Wait a minute; I know how I can get even." There is no way that we want that person who hurt us to feel good. But guess what? Forgiveness is the only way that we are going to be able to move beyond those haunting pains of our past that we keep bringing up and will not put behind us. It has been said that forgiveness is the key to freedom that will release us from the bondage of a bad past. Forgiveness is the key that will bring healing and restoration to a sick marriage. Furthermore, unforgiveness is sin, and sin can open the door to sickness. Jesus healed a woman, and then He told her to go and sin no more.

Unforgiveness can open the door to sickness

What about us? Are we sick? Are we suffering with a lingering illness? In Mark 11:23-24, God says, *"For assuredly, I say to you, whoever says to this mountain, 'Be removed and be cast into the sea,' and does not doubt in his heart, but believes that those things he says will be done, he will have whatever he says. Therefore I say to you, whatever*

*things you ask when you pray, believe that you receive them,
and you will have them."* Our focus is usually on verses 23
and 24. We talk about moving mountains if we have the
faith; however, we wonder why this mountain of sickness
is not removed. It might be that we're not practicing verse
25, *"And whenever you stand praying, if you have anything
against anyone, forgive him, that your Father in heaven may
also forgive you your trespasses."* Take some action. Ask the
Holy Spirit to search your hearts. Where are you with this? Is
there a closet that you have not been willing to open the door
to? It's time to deal with it!

Forgiveness is the key

Thirdly, we forgive because it really fits who we have
become in Christ. We are so grateful that no matter how rotten
we were, God forgave us. Those who have been forgiven the
most are the quickest to extend grace to others. It has been
said, "If we feel grateful for love given to us, we will be
generous in giving love to others." It really fits us because
Christ lives in us, and that is what He is all about.

What if we have gone through all the pain, soul searching,
and prayer and forgive that other person, but he or she does
not return our forgiveness with that same earnestness? How
do we handle this? We need to remember that the person is
not at the same place we are. That person is probably on a
different road, but because we stepped out in faith to forgive
or ask for forgiveness, we have planted a love seed into
God's garden and that will, in His time, bear fruit.

So we have taken the initial step and have come to the
place where we are ready to step out on the edge in obedi-

ence (not because we necessarily felt it) to ask for forgiveness. What is the process in doing this? I suggest that you write a letter but do not preach in it. Humble yourself before the other person. Ask him to forgive you. Write your letter with no hidden agendas. Do not expect the other person to forgive you. Ask for forgiveness, knowing full well you may not get a response of any kind.

A second area in this process is the actual healing that will help us work through the pain from merely being obedient to actually feeling forgiveness. We need to pray for that person and ask God to help us see him or her through the eyes of Jesus, with compassion and concern for them, not pity. How will we know that we are fully healed? We'll know when we can look at that person and not think bad thoughts toward them or say hurtful things — when we are actually concerned about them.

Finally, we have run the first mile as well as the second mile. We have come to grips with our bitterness, and we have walked in obedience and forgiven the pain caused by the other person. There is one final probing question: Have we really forgiven ourselves? Psalm 103:12 tells us, *"As far as the east is from the west, so far has He removed our transgressions from us."* "Forgive" means to wipe the slate clean, and He has done that for us. Since God has forgiven us, we can do no less. You may be stuck here. This is where you have to trust what God's Word says about you. You are forgiven, and it is as we read in Romans 8:1, *"There is therefore now no condemnation to those who are in Christ Jesus, who do not walk according to the flesh, but according to the Spirit."*

God's bounty is limited only by us

Begin now to invest in others, and God will change our lives. God's bounty is limited only by us, not by His resources, power or willingness to give. No obstacle, no problem is bigger than God's nature, and His nature is to bless us. I held onto one scripture no matter how lonely the nights got or how long and dark the tunnel seemed: Romans 8:28, *"And we know that all things work together for good to those who love God, to those who are the called according to His purpose."* It doesn't say all things are good. Now, don't get religious on me and try to tell me that the upsetting news you just received from your doctor is good, and you're really happy about it. Let's get real! It's all right to say it hurts. We're never going to see the way God works all this out if we're running around with a religious face, in complete denial. No, the pain, the loss, the sorrow, the debt we are going through is not good. We do hurt because of the neglect and the love we didn't receive as a child, when we wanted somebody there for us and no one came. Are you ready for this? *"All things work together for good."* The devil has tried to wipe us out, steal from us, and kill us; but God is about to turn us around. *"All things work together for good."* There is a process, and we had better get ready to witness our own miracles. It's like a caterpillar that goes into a cocoon. We can't see what's going on in the cocoon, but the caterpillar is preparing to break out into a beautiful butterfly. What really happens in that cocoon is a process.

God is getting us ready. It's a new beginning. It's a new day. He's breaking us down. He's chiseling away at our pride, anger, and the bitterness of our past, and He's pointing out all those blame games we have played. "It's his fault, not mine." He's changing the way we think, making a whole new paradigm shift. We used to think one way, and now it's God's way. We had box-like thinking. Our whole world consisted of only our territory. We don't want to come right out and say we were prejudiced, self-centered and critical, but we were. Our past may have been a security blanket for us because the way we used to handle pain was through drugs or alcohol. But now we have Jesus to handle all our pain. However, the devil wants to make us think it won't work. We have to go back to what we knew killed the pain. So God is changing the way we think. He's getting us ready because we're about to break out. We're about to witness our own miracle. Our breakthrough is now!

II Samuel 5:18-20 says, *"The Philistines also went and deployed themselves in the Valley of Rephaim. So David inquired of the LORD, saying, 'Shall I go up against the Philistines? Will You deliver them into my hand?' And the LORD said to David, 'Go up, for I will doubtless deliver the Philistines into your hand.' So David went to Baal Perazim, and David defeated them there; and he said, 'The LORD has broken through my enemies before me, like a break-through of water.' Therefore he called the name of that place Baal Perazim."* Our enemies, the past, those *inside walls* that have held us in bondage, those failures and fears that have paralyzed us — God is at work turning it all around on our behalf. He's a good God. He never stops working. He's changing us, and all that change is good. We once were in a miry bog, but God is lifting us out of the pit. It's our day. It's our time. It's our Baal Perazim — that place of break-through. He's put a song of praise in our hearts and when others see us, they will marvel at the change and will want what we have. "Just give me some of that because that's the way I want to be."

CHAPTER THREE

BE A PERSON OF VISION OBSESSED WITH COMPASSION

"...to loose the bonds of wickedness,
to undo the heavy burdens,
to let the oppressed go free,
and that you break every yoke."
Isaiah 58:6

Jesus' entire ministry was concerned with bringing salvation to the whole man — body, soul, and spirit. When Jesus looked at the crowds, I believe he saw beyond what we see today. Yes, He saw the pain and sorrow. He saw the teenager who lost hope and didn't want to live. He saw the single mom barely able to get by. He heard the cry of the parents whose doctor just informed them of the terminal illness of their child. He saw beyond the sheep to the wolf, the devil, and his angels who steal, disturb, and cast fear into the helpless mass of people, desperately in need of a shepherd. Jesus is the Good Shepherd who laid down his life for the sheep. The Bible says, *"Jesus had compassion"* (Matthew 20:34).

Paul was exhorting the church at Thessalonica when he wrote in I Thessalonians 2:7-8, *"But we were gentle among you, just as a nursing mother cherishes her own children. So, affectionately longing for you, we were well pleased to impart to you not only the gospel of God, but also our own lives, because you had become dear to us."* A young bride and mother affectionately cares for her young. I believe God is saying that His Bride, the Church, must reach out to others with that same gentle nursing care and fond affection.

God took our mess and made it a message. He drew us out of the cesspools of life and turned us around, not to be insulated and separated by four walls, but to go right back out to love, accept, and forgive somebody. You may be thinking right now, "I have failed so many times. I have had dreams and visions and goals, but I just don't know." God has a destiny for each of us, but sometimes we lose that sense of our destiny. Perhaps we forget that there is a process that leads to our destiny, and it's in that process that we are made ready for the purpose God has for us. In our process of pain and healing, we are broken. In that brokenness, God has put within us a compassion for others. The word "compassion" is an internal quality and literally comes from the word "intestines." It is a quality that God has worked into our hearts. It is the very nature of God, and all along He is getting us ready for His purpose. You're really on a journey. You are on a journey of your destiny, and what you are today is part of that destiny.

God draws His workers out of
the school of difficulties

The verses in Isaiah 58:6-12 are the very heartbeat of our Father. This is His passion, His will, and His vision for the Church. This vision is *"a great and effective door"* (I Corinthians 16:9) for the church to go through. Revelation 3:7-8 says, *"And to the angel of the church in Philadelphia write, 'These things says He who is holy, He who is true, He who has the key of David, He who opens and no one shuts, and shuts and no one opens: I know your works. See, I have set before you an open door, and no one can shut it; for you have a little strength, have kept My word, and have not denied My name."*

He is setting before the church an open door that no one can shut. *"I have set before you an open door."* This door will set the captives free. This door will bring transformation into our lives. There is no problem He cannot solve, no disease He cannot heal, no need He cannot meet. We will never be the same. We will be radically ruined for Jesus Christ.

This door will open up areas of opportunity and favor beyond our wildest dreams. This door is a vehicle for ministry that the anointing can be released through as we embrace our communities with God's love. However, we can stand before an open door forever and say, "Oh, bless God, I have an open door." But we have to step through the door. Instead, we often first want to check out what's on the other side of the door before we step through it. "But Lord, I don't know if I am really qualified." Well, guess what? We can't handle it. We need Him. Just Go. Step through the door. God will open it. We can't be stopped. It says in Revelation 3, *"...you have a little strength."* If we had a whole lot of strength, we wouldn't trust God. Right? *"...My strength is made perfect in weakness"* (II Corinthians 12:9). Church, our sufficiency is from God. When Jesus looked at the crowds, the Bible tells us in Matthew 9:36-38 that He saw how dispirited and distressed they were, and He was moved with compassion. He then said, *"Therefore pray the Lord of the harvest to send out laborers into His harvest"* (Matthew 9:38). I believe the workers are the Church. Send the Church. The doors are open. Jesus said, *"'I was hungry and you gave Me food; I was thirsty and you gave Me drink... inasmuch as you did not do it to one of the least of these, you did not do it to Me.'"* (Matthew 25:35; 45).

Pastor Jimmie Lee of El Shadai Ministries in Tacoma, Washington, recalls a lady in their South Tacoma neighborhood coming to their Saturday food distribution where she got some food to take home and made a prayer request for her family. After continuing to come for food on several Saturdays, she came to church with her son on a Sunday. On the following Sunday, she came with her husband, son, and two daughters. Then they joined the church and started attending Bible study. "Her husband started attending our Tuesday Night Men's Meeting, and I noticed that she now had a smile on her face that was not there before. She had told me when she first came to the food ministry that they were talking about divorce and were both unemployed. Now they are happily married, have good jobs, and are buying their first home. The power of a loaf of bread opened the door and Jesus totally healed this family."

The Bible says in Proverbs 19:17, *"He who has pity on the poor lends to the LORD."* The God who owns everything is saying, "You can lend to me." I said to the Lord, "But Lord, I don't understand. You own everything and yet you are saying that I can lend to you. Wow, this is humbling." The Creator, infinite, all powerful, all knowing God is saying, "John, you can lend to me. Every time you give a loaf of bread or drink of water, you lend to me." He does not say, "Oh, with your words, you lend to me; oh, with your elegant music, you lend to me; oh, with your beautiful buildings, you lend to me." The mandate from God only applies in our graciousness to the poor.

Proverbs 19:17 goes on to say, *"He will pay back what he has given."* How does the Lord repay us? So often I believe we associate this with money. But I believe it goes far beyond and much deeper than that. He will tear down the walls of the church, those things that have separated and divided us and bring unity to His Church. The Church that has been prudent, self-admiring, self-protecting, locking her doors, hiding behind her walls and speaking within her borders will become a powerful unified body of Christ to defeat evil spirits, heal sickness and disease, and relieve human burden and distresses. That Church will emerge as a hospital for the hurting, the destitute, and the outcasts — having both hands filled with bread to give to the hungry. Then the world will know that the Son of God has come in His power. Doors will be opened for the gospel. Whole families will be reconciled to His Kingdom will, and a fresh wind of transformation will blow across the land.

"I am convinced that hunger can touch anyone," says Kathryn Sokoloski. "The reality is that most of us are one crisis away from serious financial consequences that could impact our ability to feed our family. My church provided a practical, much-needed source of food, as well as emotional support and breakthrough prayer when my family experienced a crisis. They came alongside with compassion and open arms to turn my situation around. Because of their commitment to the Isaiah 58 vision and commission, we were able to move from hunger and desperation to employment and transformation."

The anointing is released

What we have in verse 6 of Isaiah 58 is the result of the anointing being released: *"Is this not the fast that I have chosen: to loose the bonds of wickedness, to undo the heavy burdens, to let the oppressed go free, and that you break every yoke?"* Verses 7, 9 and 10 describe how the anointing is released and what the chosen fast is about: *"Is it not to share your bread with the hungry, and that you bring to your house the poor who are cast out; when you see the naked, that you cover him, and not hide yourself from your own flesh? Then you shall call, and the LORD will answer; you shall cry, and He will say, 'Here I am.' If you take away the yoke from your midst, the pointing of the finger, and speaking wickedness, If you extend your soul to the hungry and satisfy the afflicted soul, then your light shall dawn in the darkness, and your darkness shall be as the noonday."*

Let's take a closer look at verse 7: *"Is it not to share your bread with the hungry..."* According to Leviticus 23:17, bread played a major role in Israel's worship during the celebration of Pentecost. Two loaves of leavened bread were offered as a sacrifice. In Exodus 25:30, the Levites placed twelve loaves of unleavened bread in the Tabernacle before the Lord each week to symbolize God's presence with the twelve tribes of Israel. It is also interesting to note that Passover is also known as the Feast of Unleavened Bread. We also know that Passover celebrates the deliverance of Israel from slavery in Egypt. Now think about it. Bread was not only symbolic of God's presence, but it was also symbolic of God's deliverance. And it was also a symbol of God's provision because throughout Exodus, God miraculously sustained the children of Israel by sending manna from Heaven each morning.

Bread – what is it really about?

Why did Jesus refer to Himself as the Bread of Life? Presence, provision, and deliverance — this is what Jesus is all about. This is the good news. Each time that you are giving a loaf of bread or a drink of water, you are being that bridge of love into someone's heart, and as that anointing is released through you, it is beginning to open people up to the Bread of Life, Jesus Christ. Not only have you helped to meet a physical need, but you helped to meet a spiritual need.

How many times have we heard it said, "Well, the real needs are in the inner city, so let the urban church take care of those needs?" If you have single moms in your church, you have a need. If you have folks on fixed incomes, you have a need. If you have people who have lost their jobs or are just not making it, you have a need. Practically speaking, dividing our bread is aimed at getting us outside of ourselves. It implies a generous attitude.

Many people in our churches today have a very low level of faith and great deal of fear. Much of this attitude has to do with our possessions. We think we have to hold on to what we have because if we don't we may not have it anymore. The underlying attitude is selfishness and fear. We have to hold on to what we have, and we fear giving it up to somebody else. It is so simple to see why God chose bread when we start receiving this bread and giving it out to others. Something supernatural begins to happen in our lives. Those invisible walls that we have constructed — walls of fear, selfishness, and greed — begin to come down. We begin to see that just as we received the bread, we receive everything else. We realize that we never had all our stuff in the first place, but somebody gave it to us, and now we're giving out what was given to us, and we're beginning to see amazing things happen in all of our lives. Our church changes, our finances change, our marriages change, our businesses change. Why? Because we are now givers and not just takers. And it all started with bread. It seems to me that when God chose to talk about the need to feed the poor so often in scripture, He was recognizing that we, the givers, have a greater need than the one we are giving to. That need is to build character in our lives. As we hand that loaf of bread to those in need, the anointing of the Holy Spirit is being released, the seed of love is being planted in the recipient, and we, the givers, are beginning to witness the anointing breaking down those walls that have kept us locked into ourselves.

There are probably people in your church who have a need but because of different reasons, they may be embarrassed to take food. Encourage them by saying, "You may not have a need but may know someone else that does, so we want to encourage you to take some food for them." This allows people to feel good about taking food and, at the same time, to maintain their dignity. Along with this, we encourage members and visitors to take food for themselves and to give out to others in their neighborhoods who may be in need, thereby becoming bridges to the hearts of others.

This is how it works, practically speaking. As Christians, we have the Holy Spirit resident in our lives, and therefore have the anointing. The Bible tells us it is the anointing that breaks off yokes and sets people free. It is the anointing that does the work. What we do when we hand out a loaf of bread is to plant a seed of love. His anointing is then released through us and begins to work in that person's life. When a second person comes along and gives out a loaf of bread to that person, the anointing is again released and the seed that had been planted is now watered. By the time a third person comes along and gives a loaf of bread to that same person, the anointing has been doing the work, walls are coming down, and doors are opening. By that simple action of compassion, the gospel is being preached.

I had the opportunity to share the way this works in a very practical illustration. I asked four people to volunteer. One man would be the non-believer who had a need for food. The other three would be the givers. The first giver planted the seed with love. The second giver watered that seed of love with more food, and the third giver brought the harvest by sharing the gospel. Unbeknownst to me, the man who was playing the role of the unbeliever had been given food by someone in that church just four weeks earlier. He came to church because of the care and compassion shown to him, got saved, and is now planted and growing. It was Mother Teresa who said, "Preach the gospel and, when necessary, use words." What the world needs now is to see our love before they hear our love.

That's vision! Once we have a vision, we need to have action with a passion to put feet to the vision. If our vision lacks action, then it becomes nothing but a fantasy.

CHAPTER FOUR

BE A PERSON OF ACTION WITH PASSION

"Is it not to share your bread with the hungry,
and that you bring to your house
the poor who are cast out;
when you see the naked, that you cover him..."
Isaiah 58:7

This has action written all over it. Action really involves two things: passion and obedience. Passion is a desire that is stronger than death, stronger than any criticism, and stronger than any opposition. If you are willing to die for your vision, then you are a passionate leader. It is passion that gets us through the discouraging times. During a time of relaxation, I was watching my favorite college basketball team play. They were down eleven points with only seven minutes to play in the game. As the cameras focused during a time-out on one young player, I noticed his eyes filled with passion and excitement. The whistle blew, and they commenced the game. What happened in those next few minutes is a testimony of what passion will do. This young man's passion ignited the whole team and, in those few remaining minutes, the game completely turned around, and they won by fourteen points. One man's passion for those few moments changed the course of that game.

Passion is Contagious

Your passion for your vision will ignite those around you. Passion is contagious. With passion, we set an atmosphere for success. Do you ever feel like giving up, but *you know that you know* that God has given you a vision? You may be thinking right now, "That used to be me. I had that kind of passion once, and nothing would stop me. But I seem to have lost it. What do I do?" I believe you need to go back to your vision and write it down where you can see it everyday. Then ask God to stir you up with the burning passion you once had in your heart, and get ready because He will do it. He is getting you ready to be a miracle in somebody's life.

Perhaps you remember the story of Elijah and the Widow at Zarephath. The Bible tells us in I Kings 17:9 that the Lord had commanded the widow to provide for Elijah. But like many of us who have heard from the Lord and have had great plans, she got distracted. She was allowing her circumstances to rob her of her mission. She said in verse 12: *"I do not have bread, only a handful of flour in a bin, and a little oil in a jar; and see, I am gathering a couple of sticks that I may go in and prepare it for myself and my son, that we may eat it, and die."* Then enters Elijah, and with these words in verses 13-14, he speaks faith into her life: *"'Do not fear; go and do as you have said, but make me a small cake from it first, and bring it to me; and afterward make some for your-self and your son. For thus says the LORD God of Israel: 'The bin of flour shall not be used up, nor shall the jar of oil run dry, until the day the LORD sends rain on the earth.'"*

Elijah was a man of God with a passion for the mission God had given him. He was there to meet the widow in her distraction and fear, and with his words he encouraged faith in her, and God gave the miracle, as we read in verse 16: *"The bin of flour was not used up, nor did the jar of oil run dry, according to the word of the LORD which He spoke by Elijah."* Many people are only an Elijah away from their miracle. Someone is waiting for you. Someone needs to see your passion and your faith. It may be a family member, a work associate, or a neighbor. Someone is waiting for you.

Obedience

This is where obedience enters in. Luke 17:5 says, *"The Apostles said to the Lord, 'Increase our faith.'"* We pray, "Lord, what I need is more faith, more faith." Luke 17:6 continues, *"So the Lord said, "If you have faith as a mustard seed, you can say to this mulberry tree, 'Be pulled up by the roots and be planted in the sea,' and it would obey you."* We run around and say, "I need more faith." But what we really need is more action. Our vision and focus may crack open windows of opportunity, but we need action to open them.

Even small faith will move mountains if we are obedient. The Bible says, *"If you have faith as a mustard seed, you can say to this mulberry tree, 'Be pulled up by the roots and be planted in the sea,' and it would obey you"* (Luke 17.6).

In Mark 4:30-32, Jesus is teaching Kingdom principles. He is saying that the Kingdom of Heaven is like a mustard seed — when sown upon the soil, though it is the smallest of all seeds, it grows up to be the largest of all trees. It is not how much faith you have. The question is, "Do you plant what you have? Do you speak it?" When you do, your faith will increase. So, the focus is not, "Increase my faith," but rather, "Increase my obedience," and an increase of your faith will follow.

What would Jesus do if he saw a hungry or a thirsty man? We know what He would do. It's written all over the Gospels. You don't need to organize a committee meeting to decide when, where, and how you are going to do it. Just do it! You come designed by God to be that person of action. This is God's very nature. He is a God of action. You were meant to fulfill your full potential. To do this you have to get out of the box. Time is running out.

How is your attitude?

As part of your action plan, check out your heart. Why are you helping those in need? When you do it, what is your attitude? The Bible tells us in I Corinthians 13:2-3, *"...and though I have all faith, so that I could remove mountains, but have not love, I am nothing. And though I bestow all my goods to feed the poor, and though I give my body to be burned, but have not love, it profits me nothing."* This tells us that we can minister to those in need without love. This means that we can be like a *"sounding brass or a clanging symbol"* (v. 1). That's an attitude that says, "I'm really great; look what I am doing. I'm here serving these poor people."

"Of course, they wouldn't be like this if they would go out and get a job." "I resent these people getting all this help, when I have to go out and earn an honest day's wages." "But this makes me look pretty good to my friends. They must think I am pretty religious, pretty caring." Have you found yourself thinking some of these self-serving, better-than-them, look-at-me attitudes? It's wrong! God says we can actually serve without love and, just maybe, we might have some of that clanging symbol in our serving.

However, think about love as it relates to our ministering to those in need. "I will be patient and kind in my serving. I will not serve in an attitude of arrogance. I will not be rude or insist on my own way. I will not resent the people I am helping. I will speak hope into their life. They can do it, I believe in them." God is a God of turnarounds. He is a God of new beginnings. It is a kind of love that says, "I just want to be your friend. I am here to encourage you, and I don't expect anything in return."

Isaiah 58 is really all about true worship. It's not just some weekly ritual but a daily lifestyle. It may begin in a church building, but it ends in the streets. What it really means is that the church gathered for worship on Sundays becomes the church scattered to LOVE on Monday through Saturday. Building believers leads to believers rebuilding their neighborhoods.

...the church gathered for worship on Sundays
becomes the church scattered to LOVE
on Monday through Saturday

One of our local churches envisioned themselves as a bridge of love to their neighborhood. They started a feeding ministry and two days a week they serve lunch to their neighborhood and even give away food items to be taken home. They are also assuring these people that they are there with a listening ear if they need to talk to anyone or need prayer for any reason.

Another church that had a passion to be that bridge to the heart is spreading love all over their neighborhood. They mow lawns, rake leaves, wash cars, clean gutters, cut wood, and buy gifts at Christmas for the children.

These Good Samaritan acts are not done to build our church. God will do that. He says, *"I will build my church"* (Matthew 16:18). We're just being those bridges to peoples' hearts, releasing the anointing, and breaking down the walls that have divided us. Trust then occurs, and when we have someone's trust, the door to his or her heart opens to allow Jesus to enter.

I'm about to do something new in your midst

I hear the Word of the Lord to the church today: "It is good, my children, that you reflect on and praise Me for where you have come. But do not get stuck in yesterday's successes or yesterday's failures, because I'm about to do something new in your midst. Some of you will have a whole new level of thinking. You have been reluctant to change. By your negative words, you even speak death into the church, into your finances, into your business, into every area of your life. That is about to change. You will begin to speak faith, hope, and life. You will begin to walk in acts of love, getting out of your comfort zones. Some of you have held prejudices. You have been jealous of others. But that is about to change, for I am a God of change; I am a God of transformation, of new beginnings. My Word says it is no longer you who lives but Christ who lives in you. You're ready to break out of those walls of jealousy, competition, pride, arrogance, fear, and independence. Your healing is about to spring forth speedily. Only look up; stop looking down. I am the God of the hills. Where does your help come from? It comes from Me. I will not allow your foot to slip. I am your refuge and strength. No weapon raised up against you will prosper. No weapon raised up against your ministry will prosper. No weapon raised up against your business will prosper. No weapon raised up against your marriage will prosper. No weapon raised up against your church will prosper. *WITH ME YOU CAN DO ALL THINGS.* You will prosper in your soul, you will prosper in your health, and you will prosper in your finances. You will prosper in your ministry. You will prosper."

This is all about taking something that is ours and giving it away. It's being that conduit for God. Growing churches are the ones that are touching people outside their four walls. An *anemic church* is a church that is turned in on itself.

CHAPTER FIVE

BE A GIVER, NOT A TAKER

Isaiah 58:10 says, *"If you extend your soul"* meaning *"if you give yourself"* as stated in the NASB version of the Bible. Giving is all about attitude. It's a heart issue. We first have to give ourselves. Philippians 2:3-4 tells us to *"Let nothing be done through selfish ambition or conceit, but in lowliness of mind let each esteem others better than himself. Let each of you look out not only for his own interests, but also for the interests of others."*

...the church needs a good funeral

What the church needs today is a good funeral. Instead of always coming to the altar for a good feeling, we need to come to the altar to die to self, to die to our pride, to die to our fears. We need to die to all our prejudices, jealousies, and competition. When we die to ourselves, we begin to see who we really are. We have to get self out of the way before we can clearly see the plans God has for us. In Jeremiah 29:11, God says, *"For I know the plans I have for you," declares* the LORD, *"plans to prosper you and not to harm you, plans to give you hope and a future"* (Jeremiah 29:11 NASB).

God's will and vision for His Church and for us is all about losing ourselves in Jesus and in others. We were born for such a time as this. We have never been more powerful than we are right now. In Isaiah 46:10 NASB, God says, *"My purpose will be established, and I will accomplish all My good pleasure."* Luke 6:38 tells us to *"Give, and it will be given to you: good measure, pressed down, shaken together, and running over will be put into your bosom. For with the same measure that you use, it will be measured back to you."* We can never out give God.

You see, one of the things about being givers is that we have to be willing to live on the edge and trust God. As long as we hang in the middle, we're comfortable and content. We're in our own little world, with our own little clique — like a groupie. But when we get out on the edge, it's not very comfortable. We even have to face our challenges. We're forging in unfamiliar territory. But this is where God wants us, because God wants givers. And, in our giving, we have to trust Him. Too many of us want to live in the middle. Let's get out of the middle and get over on the edge where we have to trust God with every step we take.

Get over on the edge

Have we grown too comfortable, too content? We may have started on the edge, but we have moved to the middle. It's been a subtle thing. It didn't just happen overnight. It's as if we just woke up and found ourselves in this comfortable place. Yes, it's secure and we're content, but it's also very boring. God is saying, "I want you back on the edge where you have to hang on to Me. I want you back on the edge, trusting Me as you give yourself to others."

Matthew 15:32-36 reads, *"Now Jesus called His disciples to Himself and said, 'I have compassion on the multitude, because they have now continued with Me three days and have nothing to eat. And I do not want to send them away hungry, lest they faint on the way.' Then His disciples said to Him, 'Where could we get enough bread in the wilderness to fill such a great multitude?' Jesus said to them, 'How many loaves do you have?' And they said, 'Seven, and a few little fish.' So He commanded the multitude to sit down on the ground. And He took the seven loaves and the fish and gave thanks, broke them and gave them to His disciples; and the disciples gave to the multitude."* Notice that Jesus didn't give out the food. He gave it to His disciples to distribute, and He gives it to us to distribute. Let's get really practical. Hold out your hands and look at them. What has Jesus put in your hands to give out? You see, my friends, we have a giver's heart when we have no hidden agendas but to give and to give and to give.

CHAPTER SIX

THE EVIDENCE OF TRANSFORMATION

A re we ready to say, "I need to get focused. I need to be a God chaser. I want to be a mover who gets out of the past. I want to be that leader obsessed with a vision and compassion. I want to be a man of action with passion. I want to be a giver that lives on the edge, trusting God?" When the WHAT of ministry and the HOW of ministry are lined up and in balance, the evidence of transformation will be the result.

EVIDENCE #1 – POWER

Isaiah 58:8, *"Then your light shall break forth like the morning."* Verse 10, *"...your light shall dawn in the darkness, and your darkness shall be as the noonday."*

I believe this is addressing depression, the number one sickness in our culture. There were times in my life when I didn't want to get up in the morning. Life was like a long dark tunnel with no light at the end. There were feelings of despair and a loss of hope. Perhaps life for us is like a tunnel, and we're dreading getting up tomorrow morning. Perhaps we have been living in that cesspool of depression where bitterness and resentment have stolen most of the joy from our lives and robbed us of our peace. Others have had hopes and dreams only to have them never to become fully realized because of all the circumstances and challenges that life had beset upon them. The Bible tells us in Proverbs 13:12 that *"hope deferred makes the heart sick."*

God says that when we are obsessed with the vision of Isaiah 58 and act upon it with that giving and forgiving attitude, the anointing will be released through us, our gloom will rise, and there will be a light that will come into our souls. Our *"healing shall spring forth speedily"* (Isaiah 58:8). That word "healing" is "recovery" in the Hebrew, meaning "restoration and power." This is a new day. It's a new season for us, so receive it now. He is Jehovah Rophe, our Healer. *"By His stripes, we are healed"* (Isaiah 53:5; I Peter 2:24). Do you want to shorten the prayer lines for healing in your churches? Then challenge God's children to quit focusing in on themselves and to start getting involved in dividing their bread and their lives with others, satisfying the needs of the afflicted, and then their own healing will break through.

EVIDENCE #2 – PEACE

Isaiah 58:8, *"...and your righteousness shall go before you."* The Amplified Bible says, *"...your righteousness (your rightness, your justice, and your right relationship with God) shall go before you [conducting you to peace and prosperity]."*

His name is Jehovah Shalom, God of peace. Everything under the sun will seek to harass you, to torment you, but Jesus said, *"Peace I leave with you, My peace I give to you; not as the world gives do I give to you. Let not your heart be troubled, neither let it be afraid."* (John 14:27). Everything can come crashing in, but we have His peace. He stands at the sea of your life where the waves are turbulent and winds are blowing, and He rebukes the winds and sea and a great calm occurs. You are covered by the blood of Jesus. The everlasting arms of our Father are under you and His glory, goodness, and mercy are following you all the days of your life. You are surrounded by His goodness. There is no problem He cannot solve. No question He cannot answer. No disease He cannot heal.

EVIDENCE #3 – PROTECTION

Isaiah 58:8, *"...the glory of the Lord shall be your rear guard."*

A good portion of the rest of our armor is frontal armor. But the enemy likes to attack from the rear at our most vulnerable place. He is a deceiver, and he seeks to attack you where there appears to be least resistance. When the anointing is released through us, the glory of the Lord protects our backs from those onslaughts of the enemy. God is our protector. He is our refuge and our strength. Before I ever leave my home in the mornings, my wife and I claim His promise of protection over our entire family. It gives us great peace and security to know that we have his complete protection, and I am convinced that there are many things that could have happened to us if we had not had His protection.

EVIDENCE #4 – PROVISION

Isaiah 58:9, *"Then you shall call, and the LORD will answer; you shall cry, and He will say, 'Here I am.'"*

He answers our prayers. He meets all our needs according to His riches. How rich is He? He owns all *"the cattle on a thousand hills"* (Psalm 50:10). When you call you need to be specific. Tell God exactly what you want Him to do, and when you are being specific, do not limit God. Ask big, because there isn't anything that God can't do. There are no limitations to His abilities. What do you need God to do in your life? Do you need a breakthrough in your marriage? Then ask the Father. Do you need help in your finances? Then ask the Father. Do you want your business to prosper? Then ask the Father. Do you need an answer to a decision that you have to make? Then ask the Father. *"Ask, and it will be given to you; seek, and you will find; knock, and it will be opened to you."* (Matthew 7:7).

EVIDENCE #5 – PROSPERITY

Isaiah 58:11, *"you shall be like a watered garden."*

When I was a boy, one of the things that I most remember is the beautiful, lush, and fruitful garden that my parents raised every year. Oh, the peas tasted so good right off the vine and, for some reason, I loved the carrots from our garden. But all of this did not just happen. My parents spent many hours in our garden doing what was necessary to produce a healthy crop. The one thing that stands out in my mind to this day was seeing my dad with his hose, spraying the garden religiously. We had a well-watered garden. The evidence of your life, as you give yourself to others in need by demonstrating love and compassion for them, will be a well-watered garden. Lush, beautiful and fruitful. You will become that Psalm 1 man who *"...brings forth its fruit in its season, whose leaf also shall not wither; and whatever he does shall prosper"* (Psalm 1:3).

EVIDENCE #6 – PURPOSE

Isaiah 58:12, *"And you shall be called the Repairer of the Breach, the Restorer of Streets to Dwell In."*

God only knows how much our streets need healing. *"Those from among you shall build the old waste places."* Historically, this is in reference to Jerusalem, which had been laid waste by the Babylonians. Walk with me for a few moments through the waste places of your communities, your cities. Families are in all kinds of trouble and disarray... divorce and child molestation are at its highest...emotional abuse, drug and alcohol addiction, and teenage suicide are at a record level...pain and more pain. Meet the battered, broken people. But we have good news! Our God reigns! Isaiah 52:7 says, *"How beautiful upon the mountains are the feet of him who brings good news."* God, who proclaims peace, who brings glad tidings of good things, who proclaims salvation, who says to our churches and our cities, "Our God reigns." Yes, God is still in the business of reclaiming and reviving cities and their people. This is what we're to be all about. This is evangelism in action. This is our purpose. This is what we are called to do in the streets of our hometowns. A young Muslim mother was given bread. Her baby was sick and was prayed for and healed the same day. Then she came to church and received Christ. As you divide your bread with the hungry, and bring the homeless poor into the house you have built — that bridge of love to the least of these — the anointing will be released and peoples' lives will be transformed by the love of Jesus. You will become known as a rebuilder of the waste places and a repairer of the breach — and a restorer of those neighborhoods in which you dwell, bringing hope and redemption to families torn apart by the stresses of life and lost in the sea of fear and hopelessness. Aaron Haskins, City Networking Pastor at The City Church in Kirkland, Washington, concisely sums up this great call and challenge to transformation: "Functional unity, reconciliation, revival, and transformation can only result from church leadership coming together as one in Christ, to reach out to the poor in our cities."

> *God is setting us apart to be those agents of*
> *healing, bringing an expression of the love of*
> *God into our hearts and into the hearts*
> *of our cities.*

Time is running out...the clock is ticking. Church, we must answer the call. We can no longer afford to get comfortable behind our four walls while the families of our communities are imprisoned in their poverty, fear, brokenness, and confusion. Rise up, O Church, for we march not to the drumbeat of this world but to the drumbeat of the Holy Spirit. Church, we must become those bridges into people's hearts, whereby the love of God is demonstrated unconditionally and those walls, both inside and outside, are destroyed. Only then will the words of our Lord Jesus, that were shared to that small band of men 2000 years ago, become a reality – *"Your kingdom come. Your will be done on earth as it is in heaven"* (Matthew 6:10).

FOOTNOTES

Introduction:

¹ Martin Luther King, *Strength To Love,* published by Harper & Row, New York, NY, 1963.

Chapter Two:

² T.D. Jakes, *Storms Don't Last Forever*, CD. No date.
³ *Merriam Webster's Collegiate Dictionary.* 10ᵗʰ ed. Springfield, MA: Merriam-Webster, Inc., 1997.

CPSIA information can be obtained
at www.ICGtesting.com
Printed in the USA
FSHW011949140921
84769FS